FORM IN ·GOTHIC

FORM IN GOTHIC

BY

WILHELM WORRINGER

———

AUTHORIZED TRANSLATION
EDITED WITH AN INTRODUCTION BY
SIR HERBERT READ

(Containing the Original Illustrations)

LONDON / ALEC TIRANTI / 1964

First English edition (G. P. Putnam's Sons Ltd.) 1927

Present edition 1957

Reprinted 1964

*Alec Tiranti Ltd., 72 Charlotte Street, London, W.*1

Made and printed in the United Kingdom

CONTENTS

LIST OF ILLUSTRATIONS

LIST OF ILLUSTRATIONS

INTRODUCTION

" Beauty is no quality in things themselves; it exists merely in the mind which contemplates them." Hume's famous saying was taken up by Kant, and a true theory of aesthetics first became possible. But Kant only pointed out the way of aesthetics; for its full development as a science many years of observation and research were necessary, and even now, so haphazard and uncoördinated has been so much of this work, that we are hardly yet in a position to define beauty or to construct a system of aesthetic values. But the necessity of a psychological ground-work has been firmly established, and it is realized that no general theory of aesthetics will be possible until the relation of the sensuous and formal elements in aesthetic perception has been thoroughly investigated. It is in Germany especially that this necessity has met with real con-sideration. The *Experimental Aesthetics* of G. T. Fechner and the *System of Aesthetics* of J. Volkelt are probably the most important con-tributions yet made to the subject. But we owe to Theodor Lipps the most fundamental psychological theories of aesthetics yet attempted, and it is as a disciple of Lipps that Professor Worringer first made his mark, with his treatise on *Abstraktion und Einfühlung* (1907).

But a further historical advance must first be noticed before we can appreciate the position occupied by Professor Worringer. This is the distinction which it has gradually been found necessary to make between " General Aesthetics " and the Theory of Art (Kunstwissenschaft). The former is concerned with all modes of aesthetic perception—with all the unorganized and disparate feelings for tone, colour, imagery, and the rest, which have nothing to do with art. Art is *ordered* expression, and the difference between art and beauty is not merely formal and historical but a difference of values. Beauty is a sensational value; art is always an intellectual value.

Professor Worringer begins with a development of Lipps' theory of Einfühlung. *Abstraktion und Einfühlung* is really an essay in General Aesthetics and forms the basis of his later essays in the Theory of Art— *Formprobleme der Gotik* (1912) and *Ägyptische Kunst: Probleme ihrer Wertung* (1927). The theory of Einfühlung has never been fully or adequately expounded in English, and it is to be hoped that some day we may see a translation, not only of Lipps' great work, but also of Professor Worringer's shorter essay. The only English philosopher and critic who has been strongly influenced by Lipps and Worringer was the late T. E. Hulme, and his summary of Worringer's essay is so succinct that I cannot do better than quote it here:

" You have these two different kinds of art. You have first the art which is natural to you, Greek art and modern art since the Renaissance. In these arts the lines are soft and vital. You have other arts like Egyptian, Indian, and Byzantine, where everything tends to be angular, where curves tend to be hard and geometrical, where the representation of the human body, for example, is often entirely non-vital, and distorted to fit into stiff lines and cubical shapes of various kinds. . . .

" It is necessary to realize that all art is created to satisfy a particular desire—that when this desire is satisfied, you call the work beautiful; but that if the work is intended to satisfy a desire and mental need different from your own, it will necessarily appear to you to be grotesque and meaningless. We naturally do not call these geometrical arts beautiful because beauty for us is the satisfaction of a certain need, and that need is one which archaic art never set out to satisfy. What from our standpoint appears as the greatest distortion must have been, for the people who produced it, the highest beauty and the fulfilment of some desire.

" Consider the difference between these two kinds, then, from this point of view.

" Take first the art which is most natural to us. What tendency is behind this, what need is it designed to satisfy?

" This art as contrasted with geometrical art can be broadly described as naturalism or realism—using these words in their widest sense and entirely excluding the mere imitation of nature. The source of the pleasure felt by the spectator before the products of art of this kind is a feeling of increased vitality, a process which German writers on aesthetics call empathy (Einfühlung). This process is perhaps a little too complicated for me to describe it shortly here, but putting the matter in general terms, we can say that any work of art we find beautiful is an objectification of our own pleasure in activity, and our own vitality. The worth of a line or form consists in the value of the life which it contains for us.

INTRODUCTION

Putting the matter more simply we may say that in this art there is always a feeling of liking for, and pleasure in, the forms and movements to be found in nature. It is obvious therefore that this art can only occur in a people whose relation to outside nature is such that it admits of this feeling of pleasure and its contemplation.

" Turn now to geometrical art. It most obviously exhibits no delight in nature and no striving after vitality. Its forms are always what can be described as stiff and lifeless. The dead form of a pyramid and the suppression of life in a Byzantine mosaic show that behind these arts there must have been an impulse, the direct opposite of that which finds satisfaction in the naturalism of Greek and Renaissance art.

" This is what Worringer calls the *tendency to abstraction*.

" What is the nature of this tendency? What is the condition of mind of the people whose art is governed by it?

" It can be described most generally as a feeling of separation in the face of outside nature.

" While a naturalistic art is the result of a happy pantheistic relation between man and the outside world, the tendency to abstraction, on the contrary, occurs in races whose attitude to the outside world is the exact contrary of this. This feeling of separation naturally takes different forms at different levels of culture. . . .

" To sum up this view of art then: it cannot be understood by itself, but must be taken as one element in a general process of adjustment between man and the outside world. The character of that relation determines the character of the art. If there is a difference of ' potential ' between man and the outside world, if they are at different levels, so that the relation between them is, as it were, a steep inclined plane, then the adjustment between them in art takes the form of a tendency to abstraction. If on the contrary there is no disharmony between man and the outside world, if they are both on the same level, on which man feels himself one with nature and not separate from it, then you get a naturalistic art."[1]

The present book, which is a translation of *Formprobleme der Gotik*, applies this theory of art in general to the explanation of Gothic art, and

[1] *Speculations*, by T. E. Hulme, London, Kegan Paul, 1924, pp. 82-5. Quoted by courtesy of the publishers.

is one of the most illuminating essays in modern art criticism. It is in the first place a criticism of the standards of all previous criticisms of Gothic art; and is then a revaluation of Gothic art in the light of an hypothesis which includes, as part of its structure, an intuitive perception or recreation of the very conditions of Gothic art—not merely the social and economic conditions, but the general spiritual aspirations of Gothic man, his world and his will. " Gothic " in this sense becomes a term of wide significance, and indeed one of the most original contributions made to the theory of art by Professor Worringer is precisely the establishment of a connection between Gothic proper and the Gothic spirit at large—the latent Gothic of early Northern ornament, for example, and the disguised Gothic of later developments such as the Baroque and certain aspects of modern architecture. This essay, then, is more than a work of psychological analysis: it is a work of imaginative insight. Not only the visible reality, but the religious and intellectual life of the Middle Ages is recreated and interpreted for our understanding. In Ruskin we are familiar with a writer who has done more than anyone else to describe the appeal of Gothic art; but Professor Worringer does more than this: he explains that appeal from the point of view of the age in which it was created. Gothic art must no longer be the romantic predilection of the traveller and archaeologist: it takes its place as the highest and most accurate expression of a great phase in the history of European culture.

Such a work necessarily makes demands on the reader: it exacts close attention and a " willing suspension " of prejudice. It also needs, in this English guise, a certain measure of forbearance. The work of translation has proved extremely difficult: for the original is written in a brilliant style which owes as much to metaphorical illustration as to logical cogency. The German is rich, animated, and at times involved; in this English rendering it cannot but appear at times tawdry, spasmodic, and confused. But there was no alternative: the thought is too exact to be trifled with, yet the expression is sometimes too individual to be rendered into idiomatic English. The result is a compromise. In the very difficult task of finding fit renderings for many of the passages, considerable assistance has been given by Mr. Bernard Rackham and Mr. W. B. Honey.

INTRODUCTION

Finally, Herr Worringer wishes me to make it clear that this work, which first appeared twenty years ago, is in many ways no longer a faithful mirror of his views. He has, of course, given his changed views expression not explicitly but implicitly in his later works, but an account of these changes of opinion could only be given in a very circumstantial manner. And in the process the inner life and movement of " Form in Gothic " would suffer. Books of this kind are living things: if you destroy their bodily unity by adding limbs to the evolved nexus of thought, you thereby destroy their breath and so their best effectiveness. This book is therefore given to English readers unrevised and uncorrected, but in the full vitality of its truths and its errors, and in the form in which, through the course of many editions, it has appealed to German readers.

HERBERT READ.

AUTHOR'S FOREWORD TO THE FOURTH
AND FIFTH EDITIONS

Once again I return this book to the printers without making any altera-
tions. It is a living portion of my past development to which I should
not care to make any patchwork additions.

If critics say anything against the plan of the book, against its manner
of developing generalizations, and against many of its details, they will,
in most cases, knock at open doors. Necessary corrections of a method
acknowledged as inadequate can only be made in later works, not by
supplementary patching of the present one.

The war, which has already kept the author nearly three years at the
front, must be the excuse for the non-appearance of such later, maturer
works.

THE AUTHOR.

On field service, February 1918.

In the sixth to the twelfth editions the number of illustrations has been
doubled. Otherwise the book remains unchanged.

THE AUTHOR.

BONN, *September 1919.*

AUTHOR'S FOREWORD TO THE PRESENT EDITION

I ask the reader of this new English edition to imagine the embarrassment of the author in his 75th year, who is faced by the question whether by the blessing of a special foreword he may newly authorise a publication which hails from the earliest beginnings of his career as a scholar. Will this reader understand that he can only resolve to do this with hesitation and reservations?

The first appearance of *Formprobleme der Gotik* goes back to the year 1910. Two years earlier was published a theoretical preamble. The title of this treatise in the psychology of style had been *Abstraktion und Einfühlung*. (Published in English by Routledge and Kegan Paul Ltd. with the title *Abstraction and Empathy*.)

 Now the author need not have published any further work on these problems in nearly half a century which has passed since the appearance of those early books, had he been convinced that the great subject which he attempted had received in this first attack an exhaustive and therefore final treatment. In fact, under various headings and on many occasions he has published supplements, revisions, corrections and amendments.

Yet nevertheless: for the general public he has remained almost exclusively the much translated author of *Abstraktion und Einfühlung* and of *Formprobleme der Gotik*. The youthful exuberance of his early works has overshadowed the continued efforts of his maturity.

Understandably, his common sense and his better knowledge do not make it easy for him to say an unreserved yes to this hasty judgment of posterity. Yet happily, there is left in him yet another authority, which finds this easier: It is his heart.

Therefore this foreword can only express how much his heart rejoices in the fact that with this new edition an opportunity is offered to a new generation of English readers, to participate in the fine venture, to be young again, together with him, the author.

WILHELM WORRINGER.

MUNICH, *May* 1956.

I

HISTORICAL METHODS

The earnest endeavour of the historian to reconstruct the spirit of the past from the materials at his disposal is at best but an experiment, conducted with unsuitable means. For however faithfully we may strive to compel ourselves to an apparent objectivity, the exponent of historical knowledge remains our own Ego with its temporal limitations and restrictions. To emancipate ourselves from the conditions of our own period, and to make our own the conditions of bygone ages to such a degree that we really think with its mind and feel with its soul, is some-thing we shall never succeed in doing. Indeed, with all our facilities for forming conceptions and acquiring knowledge of history, we remain strictly circumscribed by the limitations of our own mentality, which, in its turn, is governed by the circumstances of the time. And the more discerning, the more sensitive the historical enquirer is, the more he suffers from constantly recurring attacks of paralysing resignation to the knowledge that it is the πρῶτον ψεῦδος of all history, that past events are not comprehended and appraised from their own standpoint but from that of our own prejudices.

For the exponents of naive historical realism, doubts such as these are non-existent. Undeterred by scruples, they make the theories of their own day absolute theories for every period, and thus as it were derive from the limitations of their equipment in historical knowledge a right to a corresponding falsification of history. " These naive historians gauge all bygone opinions and deeds by the generally prevailing opinion of the moment and call this ' objectivity ': herein, for them, lies the canon of all truths; their task is to fit the past into the triviality of the present. And every method of writing history which does not accept these popular opinions as canonical, is branded by them as ' subjective ' " (Nietzsche).

Directly the historian endeavours to progress from the bare discovery and establishment of historical facts to the interpretation of these same facts, mere empiricism and induction no longer suffice. At this stage he must fall back on his faculty for divination. From the inanimate historical material at his disposal he must proceed to infer the immaterial conditions to which that material owed its existence. This is an inference in the region of the unknown, of the unknowable, for which no security, other than that of intuition, is to be found.

Who will dare to venture upon that domain which lies beyond verification? Who will have the courage to proclaim his right to hypotheses and speculations? Everyone will who has suffered from the inadequacy of historical realism; everyone will who has felt the bitterness of having to choose between two alternatives—that of resting in a certainty which pretends to be the certainty of objective truth but is actually attainable only by a one-sided, subjective forcing of objective facts, and that of giving up this ostensible security and becoming guilty of despised speculations, speculations which at least allow him to feel with a good conscience that he has got clear, as far as is humanly possible, from the rut of innate relative ideas and brought down to an irreducible residue the measure of his temporal limitations. Yielding to the pressure of this dilemma, he will prefer the conscious uncertainty of speculation based on intuition to the uncertain consciousness of the ostensibly objective method.

Hypotheses must naturally not be confounded with arbitrary fancies. By hypotheses indeed, we here mean only those broadly outlined experiments to which we are prompted by the instinct for knowledge. Into the darkness of facts, no longer explicable by the inadequate data available to us, this instinct is only able to penetrate by cautiously constructing a network of lines of possibilities of which the points of orientation can only be very roughly indicated by means of concepts directly opposite to these data. Since we are instinctively aware that all knowledge is merely indirect—fettered as it is by the time-conditioned Ego—no possibility of widening the capacity for historical knowledge exists other than by widening our Ego. Now such an extension of the field of knowledge is not possible in practice, but only by virtue of an ideal auxiliary construction of purely antithetical application. From the firm basis of our positive Ego, by means of an ideal duplication of our Ego around its opposite, we project into the boundless realms of history a more extensive sphere of knowledge. For all the possibilities of historical understanding

2

always lie upon that spherical surface spread out between our positive Ego, with its temporal limitations, and its opposite pole, the direct antithesis of our Ego, accessible to us only by means of an ideal construction. To vindicate the right to such an ideal auxiliary construction as an heuristic principle is the nearest approach to a possible suppression of historical realism and its pretentious shortsightedness. Let the results, if they must, be of a merely hypothetical character!

Hypotheses such as these bring us nearer than short-sighted realism to the absolute objectivity of history, the actual knowledge of which has been withheld from us. We thereby circle round this absolute objectivity in the widest possible curves our Ego can compass, thus obtaining the widest possible field of vision. It is only such hypotheses that can give us the satisfaction of knowing that the ages are no longer reflected merely in the narrow mirror of our positive Ego with its temporal limitations, but in that wider mirror thrown out on every side beyond the boundaries of our positive Ego. Such hypotheses in any case considerably reduce the distortion of historical reflection, even if it is a question of a mere reckoning up of probabilities.

We must repeat that these hypotheses do not sin against absolute historical objectivity, that is to say, against historical actuality, for knowledge of the latter is denied to us and its investigation may be described as a fancy with the same justice as the investigation of the existence and nature of " the thing in itself " (*Ding-an-sich*) was called by Kant a mere fancy. The historical truth we seek is something quite other than historical actuality. " History cannot be a replica of events ' as they actually were,' but only a remodelling of the actual events determined by the constructive aims of knowledge and *a priori* categories, a remodelling which makes the form, that is, the actual essence, of this kind of knowledge no less than of the knowledge of natural science, a product of our synthetic energies " (Simmel).

It is when we are concerned with those complex historical phenomena which have chiefly been generated by spiritual forces that we are most acutely conscious of the problem of the so-called objective consideration of history. In other words, it is the histories of religious feeling and of art which suffer most from our inadequate means of historical knowledge. When faced by these phenomena, the powerlessness of pure realism

3

becomes most patent. For if we endeavour to understand and estimate these phenomena by the sole light of the data available to us, we cut ourselves off from all possibilities of knowledge. Whereas, in every fact, we should here take into account the presence of spiritual conditions differing from our own, and only to be approached by the way of cautious surmise, without any certainty of confirmation. The so-called objective historical method identifies the conditions of past facts by the light of its own conditions: therefore to this method such facts become known and given quantities, while to intuitive historical research they are the proper object of investigation, and an approximate knowledge of them is all that rewards the labour of research.

As regards knowledge of the religious and artistic phenomena of the past, whilst historical realism has only given us a knowledge—a very extensive knowledge, it is true—of their outward forms, the other less self-satisfying method strives towards a living interpretation of these phenomena, and it is for this object alone that its entire synthetic energies are put to the strain.

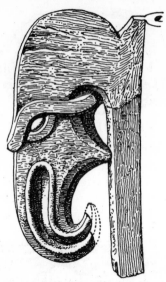

ORNAMENTAL HEAD OF AN ANIMAL
Wood-carving.   Fourth century.   Fünen, Denmark

BIRD ORNAMENT
From Codex 51 in the Library of the Monastery of St. Gall

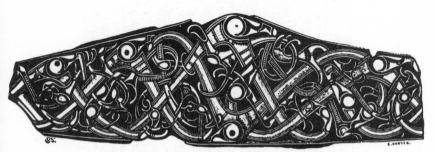

OLD NORTHERN BRONZE CLASPS
With Animal ornament.   Gotland, Sweden

(*After Salin*, Die altgermanische Tierornamentik, *Stockholm*, 1904)

Plate 1

NORTHERN FIBULA

With Animal ornament. Scania, Sweden

SOUTHERN GERMANIC BRONZE CLASP

With Animal ornament. Traunstein, Bavaria

SOUTHERN GERMANIC BUCKLE CLASP

With Animal ornament. Canton Valais, Switzerland

(*After Salin*, Die altgermanische Tierornamentik, *Stockholm*, 1904)

Plate 2

II

ART AND AESTHETICS

An attempt will now be made to arrive at an understanding of Gothic art on the basis of its own presuppositions, though clearly this can only be done by means of a somewhat hypothetical construction. Its underlying bearing on the inner history of mankind will be investigated, for that alone will enable us to grasp the creative energy of Gothic in the inevitability of its expression. For until we thoroughly understand the inevitability and the orderliness of its expression, every work of art is to us a closed book.

We must therefore seek out the Gothic will to form, that will to form which has been developed by the historical needs of mankind and which is as strongly and unmistakably expressed in the smallest crinkle of Gothic drapery as in the great Gothic cathedrals.

The formal values of Gothic have so far remained without any psychological interpretation: we must not deceive ourselves on this point. Indeed, no determined effort to estimate its positive value has ever yet been made. All attempts, such as those of Taine and his disciples, have been restricted to a spiritual analysis of Gothic man and a description of the general, historical trend of culture, without any attempt to explain the orderly connection between these subjects and the outward form of expression in Gothic. Yet the true psychology of style begins when the formal value is shown to be the accurate expression of the inner value, in such a way that duality of form and content ceases to exist.

The world of Classical art, and of the later art derived from it, has long since been the subject of such a codification of the laws underlying its forms: for what we call scientific aesthetic is nothing but such a psychological interpretation of style applied to Classical works of art. The first requirement of Classical art was held to be that concept of beauty which aesthetics, despite the diversity of its methods of approach, is solely occupied in establishing and defining. But because aesthetics applies its results to the totality of art, and believes that it has explained also those

B

artistic facts which have quite other presuppositions than this concept of beauty, its usefulness becomes detrimental, its authority becomes intolerable usurpation. A clear distinction between aesthetics and an objective theory of art is therefore the most vital necessity in a serious, scientific investigation of art. To initiate and enforce that separation was Karl Fiedler's life task, but the habit of unjustifiably identifying the teachings of art and aesthetics—a habit which dates from the times of Aristotle and which had increased and spread through the centuries—this habit proved stronger than Karl Fiedler's clear arguments. He spoke to deaf ears.

The autocratic claim of aesthetics to interpret the body of non-classical art must therefore be repudiated. For all our historical researches into art and art values are coloured by this one-sidedness of aesthetics. When we are faced with artistic facts and discover the inadequacy of our aesthetics and its concomitant idea of art as an impulse to delineate animate beauty and nature, then we value things only in a negative way. Either we regard all that is unfamiliar and unnatural as the outcome of an ability not yet adequate to its task or else, when the possibility of this first interpretation is excluded, we resort to the doubtful word " stylization," an expression of positive implication which agreeably veils the actual fact of the negative valuation.

The fact that aesthetics should have come to make this overbearing claim to universal validity rests on a deeply rooted error as to the nature of art in general. This error is manifested in the time-honoured assumption that the history of art is equivalent to the history of artistic ability, and that the self-evident, unvarying aim of this ability is the artistic reproduction and rendering of natural models. The increasing truth to life and naturalness of the objects represented was in this manner without further question taken for artistic progress. The question of the artistic will was never raised, because this will was deemed to be irrevocably settled and beyond argument. Only ability was in question, never the will.

It was actually believed that centuries had been necessary to enable mankind to learn to draw correctly, that is to say, to be true to nature; it was actually believed that artistic production takes shape from time to time only by means of a plus or minus of ability. No account had been taken of the fact, although so obvious and literally forced upon the

8

student by many factors in the history of art, that this ability was of secondary importance and that it was actually determined and governed by the higher factor of the will, which was the one and only authority.

But, as we have already said, more recent investigation into the nature of art can no longer avoid this knowledge. It must accept as an axiom that man can accomplish just as much as he wills, but that he cannot accomplish what is outside the trend of his will. Will, which formerly had not been taken into account at all, has become the real problem to be investigated, and ability, as the criterion of value, entirely disappears. For the fine differences between will and ability which really exist in the art productions of bygone times are such infinitesimally small values that they cannot be taken into consideration, particularly since from our remote standpoint their slightness can no longer be recognized and accurately estimated. For what we are always taking for the difference between will and ability when we look back in our contemplation of art, is in reality only the difference between our will and the will of past epochs, a difference which it was inevitable that we should overlook by our acceptance of the immutability of will, the valuation and establishment of which now becomes the real subject of investigation for any history of art based on the analysis of style.

Such an outlook naturally introduces into the domains of the scientific study of art a revaluation of all values which opens out immeasurable possibilities. I purposely say " into the domains of the scientific study of art," for the naive appreciation of art must not be expected to hazard in such by-roads of forced reflection its impulsive and irrational response to beautiful things. But by this emancipation from the naive outlook and by this change of attitude towards artistic facts, the scientific study of art first becomes possible, inasmuch as its valuation of the historical phenomena of art, hitherto arbitrarily limited by its subjectivity, can now first become to some extent objective.

Up to the present the classical ideal of art, as the deciding criterion of value, has been made a first consideration, and the totality of available art phenomena has been subordinated to this point of view. It is quite clear why Classical art reached this pre-eminent position—which, we repeat once more, it should, and must, always retain for the naive appreciation of art. For granted the acceptance of an immutable will,

9

concentrated on the truthful reproduction of natural models, the various Classical art epochs could not fail to appear as the height of perfection, because all disparity between will and ability seemed to have been overcome. But in reality, for us, there is as little visible difference here between will and ability as in the non-Classical epochs, and the Classical epochs possess a particular value for us only because our own artistic will is fundamentally in agreement with theirs. In our mental, as well as our artistic development, we are the successors of Classical man and his cultural ideals. In the more detailed characterization of Classical man which will be undertaken presently, in order to obtain the standard for Gothic man, we shall see in what important essentials the spiritual and intellectual constitution of Classical man coincides with the more differentiated product of evolution represented by modern man.

At any rate, it is quite clear that as the Classical epochs of art gained pre-eminence, so the system of aesthetics derived from them also reached a prominent position. All art being considered merely as a striving upwards to classical heights, aesthetics, which in reality is only an interpretation of the works of these Classical epochs in the terms of a psychology of style, was extended as a matter of course over the whole range of art. Whatever did not answer to the questions formulated by this aesthetic was looked upon as deficient and thus valued only in a negative fashion. The Classical epochs being considered as absolute zeniths, aesthetics, too, had to be credited with this absolute significance, and as a result the methods of observation in the history of art were subjectivized, according to the modern one-sided Classical-European plan. The understanding of non-European types of art suffered most from this one-sidedness. These, too, were usually appraised according to the European plan, which demands as the first requisite a truthful representation of nature. The positive appreciation of these non-European types of art remained the privilege of the few who knew how to emancipate themselves from the universal European prejudice. On the other hand, it was precisely this prejudice which, owing to the increasing intrusion of non-European art on the European field of vision due to the extension of world-relations, had helped to make evident the need for a more objective scale for the whole course of art, and to bring to view diversity of will where hitherto merely a diversity of ability had been seen.

This increased knowledge naturally reacted on the valuation of the more confined course of European art, demanding, as the first requisite, rehabilitation of the non-Classical European epochs, which so far had only received a relative, that is to say, a negative valuation from the classical standpoint. From Gothic came the most urgent demand for such rehabilitation, that is to say for such positive explanation of its forms, and the whole course of European art of the period succeeding to antiquity can really be stated as a process of adjustment between Gothic and Classic.

What is needed therefore, seeing that this existing aesthetic has only done justice to Classical art, is an aesthetic of Gothic, if such a paradoxical and inadmissible juxtaposition may be allowed without offence. Such a juxtaposition is inadmissible, because with the word aesthetic, the idea of beauty immediately creeps in again, and Gothic has nothing to do with beauty. And if we do speak of the beauty of Gothic, it is only because of the poverty of our language, which in this instance certainly conceals a very perceptible poverty in knowledge as well. The so-called beauty of Gothic is a modern misunderstanding. Its true greatness has so little to do with our current conception of art, which of necessity culminates in the idea of " beauty," that an acceptance of the word for Gothic values can only cause confusion.

Let us therefore rid Gothic of any connection with the term aesthetic. Let us strive solely for a psychological interpretation of style in Gothic works of art, which will explain to us the orderly relation between the inner sentiment of Gothic and the outward form of its expression in art; then we shall have done for Gothic what aesthetics has done for classical art.

III

THE SCIENCE OF ART AS HUMAN PSYCHOLOGY

When we look upon the history of art no longer as a mere history of artistic ability, but as a history of artistic will, it gains a significance in the general history of mankind. Its subject-matter is thereby raised to such an exalted sphere of consideration that it becomes an adjunct of that greatest of all chapters in human history, the one which treats of the development of the religious and philosophical ideas of man and reveals to us the actual psychology of mankind. For changes in will, whose mere precipitates are the variations of style in the history of art, cannot be purely arbitrary or fortuitous. On the contrary, they must have a consistent relation to those spiritual and mental changes occurring in the constitution of mankind generally, those changes which are clearly reflected in the historical development of myths, of religions, of philosophical systems, of world conceptions. Directly we have discovered this consistent relationship, the history of the artistic will takes equal right of place with the comparative history of myths, the comparative history of religion, the comparative history of philosophy, the comparative history of world conceptions: it takes equal right of place with these great stages in the general psychology of man. And thus the psychology of Gothic style will contribute to the history of the human psyche and its forms of expression.

Our knowledge of the artistic activity of man is still in its infancy as a consequence of the check it received from the one-sided classical subjective valuation previously described; and, most significant fact of all, it has not yet undergone that fundamental revolution and extension which the science of the mental activity of man owes to Kant's criticism of knowledge. The great shifting of emphasis in investigation from the objects of perception to perception itself would correspond in the sphere of the scientific study of art to a method which treats all the facts of art merely as arrangements of certain *a priori* categories of artistic, or rather, of general psychic sensibility and to a method by which these form-creating categories of the soul are the real problem to be investigated. But the further working-out of this method would necessitate the recognition of a dogma which would immediately break up again the parallelism with the Kantian criticism of knowledge, *i.e.* the dogma of the variability of the psychical categories. The plain fact is that man no more exists for the history of art than does art itself. These are merely ideological prejudices condemning any psychology of mankind to sterility and hopelessly fettering the rich possibilities of scientific knowledge. The only stable thing in the history of mankind is its actual material, the accumulation of human energies, illimitably variable, but compounded of its single factors and their resultant forms of expression.

The variability of these psychical categories, which have found their formal expression in the development of style, progresses by mutations, the orderliness of which is regulated by the fundamental process governing all development in human history: the checkered, fateful adjustment of man to the outer world. This ceaseless shifting in man's relation to the impressions crowding in upon him from the surrounding world forms the starting point for all psychology on the grand scale, and no historical, cultural, or artistic phenomenon is within reach of our understanding until it has been set in the perspective of this determining point of view.

IV

PRIMITIVE MAN

In order to describe the attitude of Gothic man towards the outer world, the peculiarities of mind and soul resulting from that attitude and the formal elements of art determined by it, we require reliable starting points and a scale of values. Gothic in its composition being an extremely complicated and differentiated phenomenon, we can only obtain a scale of values for it by first acquiring by investigation some information concerning certain original types of mankind. By original types of mankind, I mean those products of historical development in which a definite and relatively simple relationship of man to the outer world has maintained a clear and paradigmatic character. Primitive man, Classical man, and Oriental man are the great patterns which facilitate our comprehension of the less sharply defined or more finely shaded types in the history of mankind.

Primitive man, that is to say man as he was before all experience, before all tradition and history, the first link in the chain of evolution, can only be hypothetically reconstructed by us. And, in a lesser degree at any rate, the same must be said of Classical man and Oriental man who, as we conceive them, are only the unreal constructions of a roughly indicated sketch, in the sense that masses of wide extension, organically differentiated in appearance and rich in fine shades of distinction, are compelled to assume the simplicity of an ideal type. Such a reduction is permissible in historical analysis, provided the result is regarded as merely an heuristic element, that is to say, as simply the means to an end without any claim to intrinsic value.

We have a false picture of early mankind. Man's power of poetical evocation has transformed early man into a Paradisiac figure, an ideal man, the embodiment of a spiritual postulate which is animated by a vital power stronger than that of calm historical deliberation. As all metaphysical and poetic creations of mankind are but powerful and wonderful reactions of the impulse for self-preservation against the cramping, depressing feeling of human insufficiency, so the image of primeval man, the vision of mankind's lost paradise, has been given its alluring hues merely by human longing liberated from all trammels in powerful flights of fancy. The imaginative life of man is regulated by a quite primitive law: it lives by antithesis, so that fantasy provides both the beginning and the end of the history of mankind with a golden age, in which all the gloom of reality is changed into gleaming brightness and all shortcomings into wonderful achievements.

Oppressed by a vague consciousness of guilt, man has conceived the history of his development as a slow process of estrangement between himself and the outer world, as a process of estrangement during which the original sense of unity and confidence gradually disappears. As a matter of fact, the course of development is exactly opposite to this, and the original state of unity and confidence existing at the outset of development has merely a poetical and not an historical validity. We must rid ourselves of this poetical conception of primeval man and reconstruct the true primeval man by an elimination which excludes all sentimental ideas; and we must not recoil in horror from the monster which will then be left instead of the man of paradise.

If, from the sum total of the conceptions to which we cling, we deduct the enormous number of inherited and acquired experiences; if we reduce our mental patrimony to the few original elements which, in the course of centuries, have multiplied with accumulated interest beyond power of computation; if we dismantle to its very foundations the marvellously delicate fabric of the unbroken chain of transmitted characters, we are left with a creature who confronts the outer world as helplessly and incoherently as a dumbfounded animal, a creature who only receives shifting and unreliable *perceptual* images of the phenomenal world, and who will only by slow stages of progressive and consolidated experience remodel such perceptions into *conceptual* images, using these as guides for finding his way, step by step as it were, in the chaos of the phenomenal world. We must not conceive this process of spiritual and mental development of man as being a growing estrangement, succeeding to an original state of close intimacy, but as a slow dissipation of the feeling of strangeness, as a slow progress towards familiarity, by the co-ordination of all freshly visualized impressions with earlier experiences.

In any case, at the beginning of the development, there is, between man and his surroundings, an absolute dualism unmitigated by any experience. Confused by the arbitrariness and the incoherence of appearances, primitive man lives in a relationship of gloomy spiritual fear to the outer world, a relationship which is only slowly relaxed by progressive mental adjustment, and which, in spite of this relaxation, never absolutely disappears, for the dregs of these primal deep-seated experiences remain in man as a vague memory, in the form of *instinct*. For thus we define that secret undercurrent in our nature, which we recognize as the ultimate appeal of our sensations, the great irrational substratum beneath the illusory surface of the senses and intellect, to which we descend in the hours of deepest and most anguished insight, as Faust descended to the witches. And the essential content of this instinct is an awareness of the limitations of human knowledge, an awareness of that unfathomableness of the phenomenal world which mocks all intellectual knowledge. In these depths of our spiritual consciousness still slumbers the feeling of the unbridgeable dualism of existence, shattering every deceptive structure of experience and all anthropocentric delusion.

Out of this relationship of fear which is man's attitude towards the phenomenal world, there cannot but arise as the strongest mental and spiritual need the urge to absolute values, which deliver him from the chaotic confusion of mental and visual impressions. He must therefore endeavour to recast the incomprehensible relativity of the phenomenal world into constant absolute values. Speech and art, and above all the religiosity of primitive man all spring from this need. The absolute dualism of man and the world naturally implies an absolute dualism of God and the world. This timid soul, assailed by unknown forces, could as yet find no room for the idea of God immanent in the world. The Deity is conceived as being something absolutely super-mundane, as an obscure power behind things, which must in every way be propitiated and favourably inclined, against which, above all, safety and protection must be sought in every conceivable manner. Under the pressure of this intense metaphysical anxiety, primitive man brings all his acts and doings into an encumbering relationship with religion. At every step he clings fast to religious protective measures, and attempts, by means of secret exorcisms, to make himself and all that is dear and precious to him taboo, in order to rescue them from the arbitrariness of the divine powers —for so he personifies the unreliable chaos of visual impressions which withholds from him all feelings of peace and safety.

His art also is an outcome of these secret exorcising ceremonies, inasmuch as it endeavours to dam back the arbitrariness of the visual world by the intuitive creation of absolute values. In untrammelled spiritual activity primitive man creates for himself symbols of the absolute in geometric or stereometric forms. Confused and alarmed by life, he takes refuge in the inanimate, because the restlessness of life is therein eliminated and an enduring stability afforded. Artistic creation means for him the avoidance of life and its arbitrariness, it means the intuitive establishment of a stable world beyond the world of appearances, in which the arbitrariness and mutability of the latter have been overcome. He begins with the rigid line, which is essentially abstract and alien to life. Its inherent value of inexpressiveness, that is to say, its freedom from any representation of life, he dimly realizes this to be a part of an inorganic order superior to all that is living. Tormented as he is by the arbitrariness of life and its consequent mutability, it gives him peace and satisfaction, because it is for him the only attainable *intuitive* expression of the inanimate, of the absolute. He seeks further geometrical possibilities of line, creates triangles, squares, circles, places similarities together, discovers the advantages of regularity, in short, creates a primitive ornament which provides him not only with a mere delight in decoration and play, but with a table of symbolic absolute values, and therefore with the appeasement of his condition of deep spiritual distress. He employs the magic powers which, in his thoroughly logical conception, reside in these clear, stable, inevitable line symbols, by covering all his cherished belongings with these magic signs: and first and foremost seeks to make his person taboo by ornamental tattooing. Primitive ornament is an exorcism of that terror in the presence of the incoherent, surrounding world, which has not as yet been mitigated by the progressive orientation of the mind, and it is evident that a weakening of this rigid abstract character, this exorcising character of art, goes on concurrently with progressive mental orientation. Furthermore, when this capacity for mental orientation reached its highest point in the Classical epochs, and when with those epochs a cosmos was evolved from chaos, it is again clear that at this stage in the evolution of human history, art was entirely released from its exorcising character and could now unreservedly turn towards life and its organic fullness. The transcendentalism of art, the direct religious character of its values, had thus reached an end. Art becomes an ideal enhancement of life where before it had been an exorcism and a negation of life.

We will, however, not anticipate the analysis of the classical feeling towards the world and art, but return to primitive man and his art. After creating for himself a basis of absolute values, as it were by means of his linear, geometrical ornament, he endeavours still further to keep within bounds the tormenting arbitrariness of the phenomenal world; and to accomplish this, he seeks to stabilize in his perception those individual objects or impressions of the outer world which have a special meaning and value for him, and which are escaping him in the shifting turmoil of his unreliable visual impressions. Out of these, too, he attempts to create symbols of inevitableness. It is only necessary to be reminded here of the analogy of speech formation.

Accordingly, he snatches from the uninterrupted flow of events the individual objects of the outer world which he wishes to secure by fixing them intuitively. He frees them from their disquieting environment, from their forlorn condition in space, and reduces their varying modes of appearance to certain decisive and recurrent characteristics, and these he translates into his abstract linear language, assimilating them to his ornament and in this way making them absolute and inevitable. He creates artistic, that is to say, visible antitypes to the conceptual images of his mind which he has fixed in his forms of speech, and which are themselves actually slowly evolved reductions and modifications of sensuous perceptions, showing the same stenographic, abstract, and inevitable character in relation to the profusion of phenomena.

Thus for primitive man the artistic assimilation of the phenomena of the outer world is bound up with the incorporeal, inexpressive line and, in further pursuance of its tendency, with the plane surface. For the plane is the given correlate of the line, and it is only on a plane that the compact, visible embodiment of a conceptual image is possible. The third dimension, that of depth, completes the actual corporeality of the object. This dimension it is which offers the strongest resistance to the concentrated, compact comprehension and fixation of the object. For it draws it into space, and consequently into the boundless relativity of the phenomenal world. To suppress corporeal extension by translating the dimension of depth into surface dimension must have been the most immediate aim of that impulse which sought to recast into absolute and lasting forms whatever in the phenomenal world is merely relative and inconstant in space. It was only in surface representation that man in his earliest development possessed an invariable symbol for the absolute form of the individual object of the outer world, that is to say, the form which, freed from all fortuitousness of perception and from all spatial confusion with other phenomena, was withheld from him by the tri-dimensionality of the actual world.

Primitive man was only artistically active when he drew or scratched on the plane surface. If, in addition, he modelled in clay or any other plastic material, it was merely a bubbling over of playful imitative impulse, which belongs not to the history of art but to the history of manual skill. Imitative impulse and artistic creative impulse, which are here entirely separate in their nature, only unite at a very much later period of development, namely, at the time when art, no longer fettered by any transcendentalism, turned entirely towards naturalism. And the closer naturalism comes to actuality—without being in any way identical with it—the nearer in that case also imitative impulse and artistic impulse approach the one to the other, and the danger of confounding the two becomes almost unavoidable.

In spite of the peculiar suitability of two-dimensional representation for the artistic intention of primitive man as analysed above, plastic representation was not entirely outside his artistic scope. When for the sake of the enduring character of stone he occupied himself with sculpture, he sought by the most simple and unambiguous demonstration of surface relationships—by the greatest possible adherence to cubic compactness, by merely slight modifications of light and shade, that is to say, by means of a modelling that excludes all spatial, incomprehensible, fortuitous elements—to overcome the vagueness which the cubic form presents when seen from one point of view only. The result of this avoidance of any approximation to life in stylistic purpose was an approximation to abstract cubic elementary forms. Thus, the artistic representation of organic life, even in the case of sculpture, was again removed to the higher domain of an abstract, inanimate orderliness, and became, instead of a reproduction of what is conditioned, the symbol of the unconditioned, of the inevitable. But primitive man can hardly be cited as an illustration of the highest and most complicated aim of the impulse towards abstraction in art: it is only with oriental art, and more especially Egyptian art, that we arrive at any very decisive indications. But of that later.

V

CLASSICAL MAN

It is evident that the process of adjustment between man and the outer world occurs only within man himself, being nothing else but the adjustment that takes place within him between instinct and reason. In the earliest development of man instinct is still everything, reason is nothing. But supported by his increasing store of experiences and ideas, man finds an ever-growing number of fixed points in the world and the chaos of sensual impressions gradually resolves itself into an ordered arrangement of significant events. Chaos becomes cosmos. With this increasing mental mastery of the world-picture, the sense of the relativity of the phenomenal world, so derisive of all knowledge, naturally disappears; instinctive fear is allayed by objective knowledge and slowly ebbs away; and while human self-consciousness gravitates increasingly towards anthropocentric arrogance, the root of the deep-seated, unbridgeable dualism of being perishes. Life becomes more beautiful, more joyful, but it loses in depth, in grandeur, and in force. For, in the increasing security of his knowledge, man has made himself the measure of all things, has assimilated the world to his finite humanity.

For him, the world is no longer something strange, inaccessible, and mystically great, but a living completion of his own Ego, and he sees in it, as Goethe says, the responsive counterparts of his own sensations. Primitive man's vague, instinctive criticism of perceptual knowledge gives way to a joyous, self-conscious belief in perceptual knowledge, and man's rigid relationship of fear towards the world in earlier days becomes an intimate, confidential relation which liberates numerous hitherto suppressed spiritual forces and gives to art in particular a quite different function.

At this point of equilibrium between instinct and reason stands Classical man, whose best type (paradigm) is the Greek, in the ideal form in which, possibly in defiance of the actual facts, we have imagined him. He is the highest typical example for the second decisive stage in the great process of adjustment between man and the outer world which constitutes world history.

With the coming of Classical man the absolute dualism of man and the outer world ceases to exist, and consequently also the absolute transcendentalism of religion and art. The divine is stripped of its otherworldliness; it is made worldly, is absorbed into mundane actuality. For Classical man, the divine no longer exists as an exterior world, it is no longer a transcendental idea but exists for him in the world, is embodied in the world.

Man's belief in this direct divine immanence in all created things, this assumption of a world-wide and joyful pantheism, is the culmination of the world's anthropomorphizing process. · For it is this which lies concealed in such a deification of the world. The ideal unity of God and the world which has now been attained is but another name for the unity of man and the world, that is to say, for the completely accomplished subjugation of the world by mind and sense which annihilates the original dualism.

The inevitability and orderliness which primitive man, the "becoming" man, could only seek at the back of things, beyond the phenomenon itself, in the negation of life, are sought by classical man in the world itself; and as man and world are now one, are now entirely assimilated one to the other, he finds this orderliness in himself and boldly projects it into the world. Accordingly, this inevitability and orderliness, which is needed by man to enable him to feel safe in the world, is directly created out of himself. In other words, there occurs a gradual process in which religion is replaced by science, that is to say, philosophy. For to Classical man, science and philosophy are identical.

Religion gains in beauty what it loses in sovereign importance and power. Being supplanted by science, it becomes more a luxury of the spiritual life and of no immediate necessity. As we shall see later, it shares this fate with art, which undergoes a modification in character for exactly the same reasons.

In Classical man, a beautiful complementary relation exists between religion and science. The world of gods is, as it were, a sensuous correlate of the aspects of intellectual knowledge. It is true that the vague, elusive mysticism of primitive religiosity had been expelled by science,

3. Subject from northern mythology

Casket of walrus ivory, English, eighth century. National Museum, Florence

4.   Christ on the Cross
Ivory, Frankish-Alemannic, eighth to ninth century.
From Werden Abbey

5.   Miniature of St. Matthew
The St. Cuthbert Gospels, Southern English, about 770.
State Library, Munich

6.   Ornament from an Irish manuscript
Eighth century, from a Gospel at St. Gall

7. Symbol of St. Matthew
Miniature, eighth century, Echternach group.
Bibliothèque Nationale, Paris

8. The Fountain of Life
Miniature from the Bamberg Apocalypse (from Reichnau). About 1000.
(*courtesy: Akademie der Wissenschaften, Munich*)

9. Head of an Apostle
Miniature, Bavarian Book of the Gospels from Weihenstephan.
State Library, Munich

10. St. Michael
Ivory, ninth century.
State Library, Leipzig
(*After Goldschmidt,
Elfenbeinskulpturen,
Verlag Bruno Cassirer*

but the clear, sculptural quality of the Greek world of gods, in the form which had been slowly and surely developed from the fog of vague, mystical ideas, is not only in perfect accord with science, but is, as has already been said, its direct completion. The clear sculptural quality of the Greek world of gods is unthinkable without the security attained by this sensuous, intellectual insight. They complete each other as concept and perception complete each other. To the anthropomorphization evolved by science in the intellectual and sensuous domain of knowledge, there corresponds in the religious domain that creative impulse which represents the gods in human form, considering them as ideally superior human beings, who are only distinguished from human beings in degree, not in kind. Religion comes by degrees to satisfy only perceptual needs, and no longer the immediate spiritual craving for knowledge. Thus it loses its spiritual, non-perceptual, super-sensuous character.

And now, as we have already said, the artistic development runs strictly parallel to this religious development. Art also loses its transcendental super-sensuous colouring and becomes, like the Greek world of gods, an idealization of nature.

For primitive man—still mentally undeveloped and therefore contemplating the chaos of the world surrounding him with timidity and doubt —artistic activity, as we have seen, had meant the impulse to establish another world of perceptual values, a world of absolute and permanent values placed above the shifting world of appearances and free from all the arbitrariness of life. He had therefore remodelled what was living and arbitrary in his ceaselessly fluctuating visual impressions into invariable symbols of an intuitive and abstract kind. His artistic will did not arise from the enjoyment of the direct, sensuous perception of the object; instead he created precisely in order to subdue the torment of perception, in order to obtain fixed conceptual images in the place of casual perceptual images. Consequently his art bore a positive, almost scientific character; it was the product of direct impulse of self-preservation, not the unrestrained luxury product of a humanity delivered from all elemental world fears.

Art became this beautiful, stately product of refinement in the classical periods of human development. Classical man no longer suffered from the torturing relativity and uncertainty of the world of appearances, from the torments of perception endured by primitive man. The regulating and adjusting activity of his mind had sufficiently controlled the arbitrariness of the phenomenal world to give free play to his enjoyment of life. The creative energies of his spirit, liberated from the immediate necessity of mental self-preservation, were freed for a more joyous, realistic activity, for art in our sense of the term, the sense in which art and science stand in absolute opposition. As universal piety, according to Goethe's meaning, developed from universal fear, so a vital impulse for empathy [1] developed from a powerful impulse for abstraction. With all his senses, Classical man devotes himself to the sensuous world of appearances, in order to remodel it after his own image. There is no longer anything inanimate for him; he animates all things with his own life. To him artistic activity means fixing in visible form the ideal process whereby he accords his own sensibility to the living world around him; he no longer avoids the casualness of phenomena but merely chastens them to an organically smooth orderliness: in other words, chastens them by means of the indwelling counterpoint of his own feeling for life of which he has become joyously aware. Every artistic representation now becomes as it were an apotheosis of this elementary feeling for life of which he has grown conscious.

The feeling for beauty in living things, for the joy-inspiring rhythm of the organic world, has awakened. Ornament, which formerly was just orderliness, not expressing anything but the inevitable, the invariable, and therefore without any direct expression at all, now becomes a living, energetic movement, an ideal play of organic tendencies freed from all purpose. It resolves itself entirely into expression, and this expression is the life lent by man from his own store of vitality to forms which are inanimate and unmeaning in themselves. This transference of feeling (empathy) reveals to Classical man the pleasures of contemplation, which,

---

[1] " Empathy " has already been adopted as a translation for *Einfühlung* on the analogy of " sympathy." Empathy implies a transference of feeling from the subject *into* the object and as such is the antithesis to abstraction, which implies the withdrawal of all elements of subjective feeling from the object of perception. For a complete exposition of this antithesis and the theory of aesthetics based on it, the reader should refer to Professor Worringer's *Abstraktion und Einfühlung*. [ED.]

in the first rough, partial adjustment to the objects of the surrounding world, had so far been denied to the mentally undeveloped man.

At this Classical stage of human development, creative art consists in the ideal demonstration of conscious and chastened vitality; it becomes an objectified sense of one's enjoyment. Freed from all dualistic memories, man celebrates, in art as in religion, the realization of a felicitous state of spiritual equilibrium.

VI

ORIENTAL MAN

In the sphere of Western culture Classical man, with his well-balanced state of mind, represents a culminating point. In him is embodied the ideal standard of Western possibilities. But we must not confound Europe with the whole world: we must not, in our European awareness, allow our eyes to be blind to the phenomenon of Oriental culture, which almost surpasses our limited powers of imagination. For, on contemplating Oriental man, this third great typical specimen of the development of mankind, there is forced upon us an entirely fresh standard of values in human development, which corrects our hasty European judgment. We are obliged to admit that our European culture is a culture of the mind and the senses only, and that by the side of this culture of mind and senses, which is associated with the fiction of progress, there exists another, nourished by deeper kinds of knowledge than that of intellect, nourished above all by that one most valuable kind derived from instinct; we have to admit that those intellectual types of knowledge are null and void and mere superficial sham. Oriental culture is once more built up on instinct and the cycle of development is complete. The Oriental is far nearer to primeval man than is Classical man, and yet a whole cycle, an entire world of development, lies between them. The veil of Maya, before which primeval man stood in vague terror, has been drawn aside by the Oriental, who has looked into the face of the inexorable dualism of all being. His deep-rooted instinctive knowledge of the ambiguity of appearances and of the unfathomable enigma of being leaves no room for the rise of that naive belief in the value of this present state, from which Classical man had derived so much satisfaction. That happy amalgamation of sensuous feeling and intellectual knowledge which had led Classical man simultaneously to a rendering perceptible, that is to say, to a humanization as well as to a rationalization, of the world, was an impossibility to Oriental man, because of the absolute predominance of his instinctive knowledge over his outer or empirical knowledge. The

35

realm of the Oriental soul remains absolutely untouched by the progress of intellectual knowledge; the two do not blend but only stand side by side: without equality of value or commensurability. Intellectual knowledge might reach a certain stage, but it could never become a productive element of culture after the Greek fashion, for it lacked spiritual anchorage. All productive culture-creating energies were rather bound up with instinctive knowledge.

This instinctive knowledge again brings Oriental man close to primitive man. The same fear of the world, the same need for liberation lives in him, just as it did in man of the first phase of the development. But with this difference, that in Oriental man all this is not something preliminary which recedes before growing intellectual knowledge, as it did in primitive man, but a stable phenomenon, superior to all development, which is not *before* all knowledge but *beyond* it. If, in contradistinction to the Classical European man and his anthropocentric mode of thought, the human self-consciousness of the Oriental is so small and his metaphysical submissiveness so great, it is because his world-sensibility is so great.

The dualism of the Oriental is superior to knowledge. He is no longer confused and tormented by this dualism, but feels it as an exalted destiny and humbles himself silently and without desire before the great impenetrable secret of being. His fear has been chastened into worship, his resignation has become a religion. Life for him is no confused and tormenting senselessness, but is holy, because it is rooted in depths which are inaccessible to man, making him sensible of his own nullity. For this feeling of his nullity exalts him, because thereby life maintains its greatness.

The dualistically fettered world-sensibility of the Oriental is clearly reflected in the strictly transcendental complexion of his religion and of his art. Life, the phenomenal world, reality—in short, everything which Classical man in his naively joyous innocence valued as being positive—in the more profound Oriental knowledge of the world becomes consciously relative again and subjected to a higher appraisement, which is itself determined by a higher reality than exists in this world. This conception of a Beyond imparts to Oriental metaphysics a dynamic tension unknown to the Classical world in its maturity, and, as if in answer to this spiritual tension, there arises of necessity the thought of redemption, in which Oriental mysticism culminates and which, in Christianity, finally takes on what is for us its most familiar stamp.

Oriental art is the same response to the same tension. It also exhibits an absolute redemptive character, and its sharply outlined, transcendentally abstract complexion divides it from all that is Classical. It expresses no joyful affirmation of sensuous vitality, but belongs rather entirely to the other domain, which through all the transitoriness and chances of life strives for a higher world, freed from all illusions of the senses, from all false impressions, a domain in which inevitableness and permanency reign and to which the great serenity of Oriental instinctive knowledge gives its consecration.

The art of the East, like that of primeval man, is strictly abstract and bound to the rigid, expressionless line and its correlate, the plane surface. But in the wealth of its forms and the congruity of its solutions, it far surpasses primitive art. The elementary creation has become a complicated artistic form: primitiveness has become culture and the higher, more matured quality of world-sensibility reveals itself in an unmistakable manner, in spite of the outward sameness of the medium of expression. We do not, as a general rule, fully appreciate the great difference between primitive and Oriental art, because our European vision is not trained to detect nuances in abstract art, and because we only see what they have in common, that is to say, only the unlifelikeness, the remoteness from nature. In reality, there is just as much difference between them as there is between the vague fetishism of primitive man and the profound mysticism of Oriental man.

VII

THE LATENT GOTHIC
IN EARLY NORTHERN ORNAMENT

Having briefly described the three principal types of human development, that is to say, the main features of the three principal stages in the
process of adjustment between man and the outer world, we will approach
from these fundamental points of orientation our real problem—Gothic
art.

It must at once be said that the psychological conception of the Gothic
style, as it will be revealed by our investigation, in no way coincides with
historical Gothic. That more limited Gothic, which has been determined by the academic use of the term, we conceive rather as merely the
final result of a specifically northern development which had already
appeared in the Hallstadt and La Tène period, and its ultimate roots even
earlier. The principal field of this development, which may have
originated in Germanic Scandinavia, lies chiefly in Northern and Central
Europe.

In other words, when the psychologist of style, faced with the matured,
historical Gothic, has once grasped the basic character of the Gothic
will to form, he can detect this will to form as being active underground,
as it were, even where, obstructed by more powerful external conditions
and hindered in its free expansion, it assumes a foreign disguise. He
recognizes that this Gothic will to form dominates, not externally but
internally, Romanesque art, Merovingian art, the art of the Migration
period, in short the whole course of Northern and Central European art.

It is the real aim of our investigation to provide justification and proof
for this wider connotation of the stylistic term Gothic. For the present
this assertion which we are endeavouring to establish may be put forward
merely as a thesis.

We repeat, then, that in our opinion the art of the entire Western
world, in so far as it had no direct share in antique Mediterranean culture,

was in its inmost essence Gothic and remained so until the Renaissance, that great reversal of the Northern development: that is to say, its immanent will to form, often scarcely to be recognized in its outward expression, is the very same which was to receive its clear, untroubled, and monumental expression in mature historical Gothic. Later on we shall see that even the Italian Renaissance, which proceeded from totally different spiritual premisses, when it invaded the North and became the European style, was unable entirely to suppress this Gothic will to form: in a certain sense, Northern Baroque is a flaring up again in a strange garb of the suppressed Gothic will to form. And so Gothic, as a term in the psychology of style, also extends beyond the period implied in the academic use of the term, right down to the present day.

The basis on which the Gothic will to form develops is the geometrical style, which, as the style peculiar to primitive man, is spread over the whole earth; but at the period when the North enters into the historical development, this style appears as peculiarly the common property of all Aryan peoples. Before describing the development of this primitive, geometrical style into Gothic, we should like to indicate the situation as regards world history by recalling that already at the time of the Doric migration this universal Aryan style was in conflict with the style of the early Mediterranean peoples, in which there was a certain element of orientalism, and that it gave the impetus to the specifically Greek development. At first, the conflict between the two heterogeneous styles of thought is wholly confused: the Mycenean style and the Dipylon style. Then it is repeated in a milder form in the characteristic differences between Doric and Ionic. Finally the two are reconciled in the matured classical style; in short, this first offshoot of the Aryan style disappears entirely in the Mediterranean culture: and so it ceases for the present to claim our attention.

Our interest is centred on the conglomeration of young, still undeveloped groups of peoples in Northern and Central Europe, which had not, as yet, come into contact with the higher Mediterranean culture, itself dependent on the East, and in which, on the basis of the general Aryan geometrical style, there was developing the great, future force of the Middle Ages— Gothic.

In this Northern and Central European conglomerate of nations, the

39

real breeding ground of the Gothic style, we will not single out any nation in particular as being the exponent of this development: if, however, we subsequently speak chiefly of Germanic development, it will not be in any spirit of race-romanticism such as that of Houston Stewart Chamberlain, but more for convenience' sake and from the consciousness that, in this chaos of Northern peoples above all, differences in race are so far outbalanced by community in conditions of life and state of spiritual development, that it is entirely justifiable to cite one single nation as *pars pro toto*. On the other hand, thus to cite the Germanic peoples in particular is in any case in accordance with our view that a disposition to Gothic is only found where Germanic blood has mingled with that of the other races. The Germanic peoples are therefore not the sole exponents of Gothic nor its sole creators: Celts and Latins have an equally important share in Gothic development. But probably a Germanic strain is the *conditio sine qua non* for Gothic.

In contrast to the exactness proper to detailed investigations, it will not be necessary, in the broader framework of our proposed study, to take such meticulous notice of the differences existing between the individual exponents of the general Northern development.

The art of this Northern conglomeration of peoples, at the time when it waited as it were for the downfall of the Roman Empire as its cue for assuming its position of principal actor in the historical development of the world, was merely ornament. And at first, this ornament is indeed purely abstract in character. All attempt at a direct reproduction of nature is lacking. Haupt, the authoritative historian of Germanic art, says of early Germanic ornament: " In their art, there is no representation of nature, either of man, animals, or trees. Everything has become surface decoration. Therefore, as far as these races are concerned, we cannot speak of an actual pictorial art in the modern sense of the word: art in the sense of an attempt to imitate anything whatsoever that is before their eyes does not even exist." It is, then, a purely geometrical interplay of lines, although by using the word interplay we do not wish to associate with this kind of art activity any character of playfulness. On the contrary, from our preceding remarks concerning primitive ornament, it is quite evident that this early Northern ornament also has a strong metaphysical content.

In its earliest periods it is not essentially different from the primitive geometric style which we have established as common to all Aryan races. But on the basis of this elementary Aryan grammar of line, a particular linear language gradually developed, which clearly revealed itself as being a specifically Germanic idiom. It is the linear fantasy which, in the terminology of the materialistic theory of art, is described as interlaced ribbon or plaited ornament. To whatever spot the Germanic races were dispersed by the upheavals of folk migrations, there we find in their graves this peculiar and quite unmistakable ornament—in England, in Spain, in North Africa, in Southern Italy, in Greece, and in Armenia.

Lamprecht describes this kind of ornament in the following words:

" There are certain simple motives whose interweaving and commingling determines the character of this ornament. At first there is only the dot, the line, the ribbon; later the curve, the circle, the spiral, the zigzag, and an S-shaped decoration are employed. Truly, no great wealth of motives! But what variety is attained by the manner of their employment! Here they run parallel, then entwined, now latticed, now knotted, now plaited, then again brought through one another in a symmetrical checker of knotting and plaiting. Fantastically confused patterns are thus evolved, whose puzzle asks to be unravelled, whose convolutions seem alternately to seek and avoid each other, whose component parts, endowed as it were with sensibility, captivate sight and sense in passionately vital movement."

We have here a linear fantasy whose basic character we must endeavour to analyse. As in the ornament of primitive man, the vehicle of the artistic will is the abstract geometrical line, which embodies no organic expression, that is to say, no possibilities of organic interpretation. Whilst, however, it is in the organic sense *without* expression, it is nevertheless of the utmost vitality. Lamprecht's words expressly bear witness to the impression of passionate movement and vitality, a questing, restless tumult in this confused medley of lines. Since line is lacking in all organic timbre, its expression of life must, as an expression, be divorced from organic life. It is therefore necessary to understand the peculiar nature of this super-organic mode of expression.

We see that, in spite of its abstract linear character, Northern ornament gives rise to impressions of vitality which our own vital feeling, necessarily

41

projecting itself into the object of perception, would *immediately* attribute solely to the organic world. This ornament seems therefore to unite the abstract character of primitive geometrical ornament with the vital character of Classical ornament, with its organic complexion. But this is not the case. It can in no way claim to represent a synthesis, a union of these elementary contrary principles: it would be more correct to describe it as a hybrid phenomenon. This is not a case of the harmonious inter-penetration of two opposite tendencies, but of an impure, and to a certain extent uncanny, amalgamation of them, a requisition of our capacity for empathy (which is bound up with organic rhythm) for an abstract world which is alien to it. Our organically tempered sense of vitality recoils before this senseless rage of expression as from a debauch. When, however, finally yielding to compulsion, its energies flood these lifeless lines, it feels itself carried away in a strange and wonderful manner and raised to an ecstasy of movement, far outstripping any possibilities of organic movement. The pathos of movement which lies in this vitalized geometry—a prelude to the vitalized mathematics of Gothic architecture —forces our sensibility to an effort unnatural to it. When once the natural barriers of organic movement have been overthrown, there is no more holding back: again and again the line is broken, again and again checked in the natural direction of its movement, again and again it is forcibly prevented from peacefully ending its course, again and again diverted into fresh complications of expression, so that, tempered by all these restraints, it exerts its energy of expression to the uttermost until at last, bereft of all possibilities of natural pacification, it ends in confused, spasmodic movements, breaks off unappeased into the void or flows senselessly back upon itself.

When contemplating Classical ornament in its organic purity and moderation we feel as if it sprang naturally from our own sense of vitality. It has no expression but the one we give it. On the other hand, the expression of Northern ornament does not directly depend upon us; we are met rather by a vitality which appears to be independent of us, which challenges us, forcing upon us an activity to which we submit only against our will. In short, the Northern line does not get its life from any impress which we willingly give it, but appears to have an *expression of its own*, which is stronger than our life.

42

THE LATENT GOTHIC IN EARLY NORTHERN ORNAMENT

We must endeavour to obtain a more intimate understanding of this specific expression of the Northern, that is, Gothic line, which, in a strict psychological sense, is naturally only apparent. We will fall back on commonplace experiences of daily life. If we take a pencil and scribble unmeaning lines on paper, we can soon realize the difference between the expression dependent upon us and the specific expression of the line which is seemingly independent of us.

If we trace a line in beautiful, flowing curves, our inner feelings unconsciously accompany the movements of our wrist. We feel with a certain pleasant sensation how the line as it were grows out of the spontaneous play of the wrist. The movement we perform is of unrestrained facility: the impulse for movement once given is continued without effort. This feeling of pleasure, this freedom of formation, is now unconsciously transferred to the line itself, and what we have felt in executing it, we ascribe to it as expression. In this case, then, we see in the line the expression of an organic beauty because the execution of the line was in conformity with our organic feelings. If we meet such a line in another composition, we experience the same impression as if we ourselves had drawn it. For directly we admit a line to our consciousness at all, we unconsciously feel inwardly the process of its formation.

Besides this organic capacity for expression in the line of which we are conscious in all Classical ornament, there exists yet another, which is the one to be considered in our Gothic problem. Once more we must fall back on the commonplace experiences of playful line scribbling. If we are suffering from great mental stress, which cannot be otherwise expressed than on paper, the scrawled lines will turn out to be quite different. The will of our wrist will certainly not be consulted: the pencil will move wildly and violently over the paper and instead of the beautiful, round, organically tempered curves, there will be a hard, angular, ceaselessly interrupted, jagged line, of the most powerful vehemence of expression. It is not the wrist which spontaneously creates the lines, but our violent will for expression which imperiously compels the wrist movement. Once the initial impulse for motion has set in, it cannot be allowed to follow its natural tendency to run out of its own accord, but must always merge into a renewed impulse for movement. If we admit such a line, born of such excitation, into our consciousness, we have even in its case

43

an unconscious reflex feeling of the process of its origin. But in this case this reflex sensation is not accompanied by any feeling of satisfaction, for we have an impression that we are being coerced by some alien, imperious will. We are made aware of all the processes of suppression of the natural tendency for movement. At every break, at every change of direction, we feel how the forces suddenly checked in their natural course are blocked; how, after this instant's arrest, they pursue, with a momentum increased by the obstruction, a new direction of movement. And the more frequent the breaks, the more numerous the obstacles, the more powerful will be the impetus at the points of rupture, the more forceful every time will be the onrush in the new direction; in other words, the mightier and more impetuous will be the expression of the line. For here, too, we ascribe to the line as expression the sensation of the process of its execution felt afterwards at the moment of its apperception. And as the line appears to impose its expression upon us, we perceive it as something absolute, independent of us, and therefore we speak of a specific expression of the line.

The essence of this specific expression of the line is, that it does not represent sensuous, organic values, but values of a non-sensuous, that is to say, a spiritual kind. It does not express organic activity of will, but a psychical, spiritual activity of will, far removed from any connection or conformity with the complexes of organic sensation.

In advancing these opinions, we do not mean that Northern ornament, that " almost primeval and gloomy chaotic confusion of line " (Semper), is on a level with the lines scrawled by a man who is psychically or mentally excited, nor that it is only a reflection on a large scale of this phenomenon of everyday experience. That would be to make comparisons between quite incommensurable entities. Nevertheless, this comparison gives us hints. Just as those scribbled lines appear to be only the outlet for an inner spiritual oppression, the excited, jerky feverishness of the Northern line undoubtedly throws a striking light on the heavily oppressed inner life of Northern humanity. This comparison enables us at any rate to establish the expression of spiritual unrest in Northern ornament. But what, in ordinary daily life, appears to be a playful scribble of lines, assumes a different complexion when considered as the artistic expression of a whole race: in this case, it becomes a longing to

44

be resolved into an unnatural, intensified activity of a non-sensuous, spiritual kind—one is here reminded of the labyrinthine scholastic mode of thought—and, in this exaltation, to be freed from the direct feeling of thraldom to reality. And, to anticipate, it was this longing for a non-sensuous activity, exalted above all senses, or to use the correct word, a super-sensuous activity, which created this ornament lashed into the utmost degree of expressiveness; it was the same which brought into being that transcendentalism in stone—the Gothic cathedral.

While Gothic architecture presents a picture of the complete de-materialization of stone, and is full of spiritual expression unrestrained by stone and sense, early Northern ornament presents the picture of a complete de-geometrization of line for the satisfaction of the same needs of *spiritual* expression.

In primitive ornament the line is geometrical, lifeless, and void of expression. Its artistic significance rests solely and entirely on this absence of life, on its utterly abstract character. With the decrease of the initial dualism between man and the world, that is to say, with the spiritual development of mankind, the abstract, geometrical character of the line gradually weakens. This weakening, this transition from rigid inexpressiveness to complete expressiveness, may manifest itself in two different directions: lifeless geometrical being may be replaced either by an organic vitality, pleasing to the senses—as happens in Classical ornament—or else by a spiritual vitality, extending far beyond the senses, as in the early Northern ornament, the Gothic character of which we have thus already established. And it is evident that the organically determined line contains beauty of expression, while power of expression is reserved for the Gothic line. This distinction between beauty of expression and power of expression may at once be transferred to the whole character of the stylistic phenomena of Classical and Gothic art.

11.   The Incredulity of St. Thomas
Ivory book cover, about 990, Echternach Group.
From the Figdor Collection
(*After Goldschmidt, Elfenbeinskulpturen, Verlag Bruno Cassirer*)

12. Descent from the Cross
Ivory, Spanish, eleventh century.
Victoria & Albert Museum, London

13. Evangelist
Miniature, from a Gospel book formerly at Altomünster,
twelfth century.   State Library, Munich (Clm. 2938)

14. Evangelist
Miniature, from a Gospel book formerly at Altomünster,
twelfth century.   State Library, Munich (Clm. 2939)

15. Capital of a twin column, twelfth century.
From the abbey of Sainte-Marie-la-Daurade, Toulouse
(photo: Giraudon, Paris)

16.   Richly decorated column.
From the Abbey Church of Coulombs,
now in the Louvre
(*photo: Dr. George Zarnecki*)

17.   Christ on the Cross.
Detail of bronze, beginning of twelfth century, from Werden Abbey

18. Bell cover.
Embroidery, thirteenth century.   From the Abbey of Melk

VIII

THE CEASELESS MELODY OF
NORTHERN LINE

The antithesis between classical ornament and Northern Gothic ornament requires a more exhaustive consideration. The fundamental difference in the character of these two manifestations of art must also be demonstrated in detail. When comparing the two styles of ornament, the first point that strikes one is that Northern ornament lacks the concept of symmetry which from the beginning was so characteristic of all Classical ornament. Symmetry is replaced by repetition. It is true that repetition of a single motive plays its part in Classical ornament also: but such repetition is of an entirely different nature. In Classical ornament there is a general inclination towards repetition of the selected motive the opposite way round, as if in a mirror, thereby avoiding the appearance of endless progression produced by repetition. By repetition of this reversed kind, a feeling of serenity, of completion in the rhythm, is created; this successive arrangement gives an effect of restful addition which never mars the symmetry. By a structure of pauses, the organically guided sensibility of Classical man gave ever-recurrent accents of rest to the movement derived from repetition, a movement which threatened to pass beyond the organic measure and become mechanical. By this repetition in reverse order, demanded by the organic feeling, the hurrying, mechanical activity is, as it were, bridled.

On the other hand, in Northern ornament repetition does not bear this restful character of addition, but has, so to speak, a character of multiplication. The intervention of any desire for organic moderation and serenity is here lacking. A continually increasing activity without pauses or accents is set up and repetition has only the one aim of giving the particular motive a potential infinity. The infinite harmony of the line hovers before Northern man in his ornament: that infinite line which gives no pleasure, but which stuns and compels us to helpless surrender.

FORM IN GOTHIC

If, after contemplating Northern ornament, we close our eyes, all that remains to us is a lingering impression of a formless, ceaseless activity.

Lamprecht speaks of the enigma of this Northern intertwining ribbon ornament which one would like to investigate. But it is more than enigmatical: it is labyrinthine. It seems to have neither beginning nor end and above all no centre: there is a total absence of any such means of guidance for the organically arrested feeling. We find no point of entrance, no point of rest. Every point in this endless movement is of equal value and all of them combined are without value compared with the agitation they produce.

We have already said that the endless activity of Northern ornament is identical with that which Gothic architecture later wrested from the inanimate masses of stone, and this comparison is but confirmed and made clear by the establishment of a difference. For while the impression of endlessness of line could only be attained if it really had no visible end, that is to say, if it vanished unmeaningly into itself, in architecture the impression of endless movement was attained by the exclusive accentuation of the vertical.

When we turn to this movement, converging on all sides to escape in an upward direction, its actual termination in the highest point of the tower need not be considered at all: the movement repeats itself endlessly. Here the vertical accentuation indirectly produces the symbol of infinity, which in the ornament is directly produced by the return of the line into itself.

We have therefore established, not only the predominantly asymmetrical peculiarity of Northern ornament, but also its predominantly acentric quality. But this determination only concerns the general character; in details, exceptions occur. For, in the North, there are a number of ornamental motives which have an undoubted centric character, but here too we note a decisive difference if we compare similar Classical ornament. For example, instead of the regular and invariably geometrical star or rosette or similar restful forms, in the North we find the revolving wheel, the turbine or the so-called sun wheel, all designs which express violent movement. Moreover, the movement is peripheral and not radial. It is a movement which cannot be arrested or checked. " While with its opposed—negative and positive—movement inwards towards the centre or from the centre outwards, classical ornament terminates within itself, thereby bringing itself to complete rest, northern ornament, beginning at a given point, moves ever further forward in the same direction until it has covered the whole surface and returns as a natural consequence to itself " (Haupt). The difference between the radial movement of antique and the peripheral movement of Northern ornament is therefore quite similar to that between simple repetition and repetition with counterchange. In the one case there is quiet, measured organic movement; in the other, the uninterrupted, accelerating, mechanical movement. And we saw how, on closer investigation, it is precisely in an apparent relationship between the laws of formation of classical and Northern ornament that their difference is all the more clearly defined.

IX

FROM ANIMAL ORNAMENT TO HOLBEIN

If, in the course of its development, the organic flow of Classical ornament gradually loses its general bearing and inclines towards the particular, that is to say, if it takes unto itself from nature unusually significant embodiments of organic law as ornamental motives, it is a perfectly natural spontaneous proceeding. Instead of reproducing the latent law of natural forms, the classical artist now reproduces these natural forms themselves not by mere naturalistic copying, but with complete realization of their ideal character. He only makes ideal epitomes of them, but these suffice to make the law of organic form perceptible. The vegetable world alone could provide him with the organic law of form in the pragmatic purity he desired: therein he found a kind of grammar of the organic laws of form, and it was clear that having until then only spoken as it were by signs, that is to say, in organically vibrating, organically rhythmed linear motives, he now learned, by basing himself on this natural grammar, to express himself in a more direct, more supple, more lively, and varied fashion. In short: the plant motives of classical ornament are a natural outcome of their organic basis.

The animal motives of Northern ornament are quite a different matter. They are not naturally and spontaneously evolved from the nature of Northern linear drawings, but belong to an utterly different world and in conjunction with these drawings they impress us as being absurd and enigmatic. No comparison between the character of classical plant ornament and the character of the Northern animal ornament can be made. Their genesis, their meaning, and their aim differ fundamentally and are utterly incommensurable. We need only examine Northern animal ornament somewhat more closely to be aware of the impossibility of comparing its peculiarities with classical values.

At the beginning of this investigation concerning ornament, we had established that Northern ornament bore a purely abstract character and that it exhibited no representation of natural prototypes. This statement is hardly affected in any essential manner by the presence of this animal ornament. For this animal ornament is not the result of a direct observation of nature: it is composed of imaginary shapes, evolved more or less arbitrarily from the linear fantasy, and without which they do not exist. It is a playing with memories of nature within the limits of this abstract linear art, without any aim of distinctness such as would be proper to the observation of nature. Haupt says: " The animal world is absorbed into the network, not as an imitation of nature, but simply as a surface decoration. The animal seems to have a head, one or two feet, its body is wound in and out like that of a snake; sometimes the available surface is covered, as in a carpet, by a design representing several animals of the same kind woven together in a plaited knot, and it is only an experienced eye which can detect whether these are meant to be actual pictures of animals or not. The casual observer sees the whole simply as a plaited pattern. If at the points and ends actual portions of limbs are introduced, they are so much divided and adorned and concealed by lines and notches that they can hardly be recognized as what they originally were."

This animal ornament may consequently have sprung from distant memories of animal forms being awakened by certain purely linear forms and by these memories (for certain reasons to which we shall return later) being followed up by increasing and emphasizing the similarity, perhaps by indicating eyes with dots or by something of that kind,—all this without detracting in any way from the purely abstract linear character of the ornament. That these designs were based upon recollections not of any definite species but of animals in general is proved by the fact that motives from widely different animals were thoughtlessly combined. It was only later naturalization that made these shapes develop into these well-known, fabulous monsters which were adopted in later ornament with more predilection than understanding. Originally these shapes were merely the offshoots of a *linear* fantasy: apart from this linear fantasy they have no existence, not even in the imaginative life of Northern man.

We said that, together with these fabulous animal forms, distorted recollections of nature crept into the abstract play of line. That is, however, not absolutely correct. For, in this case, it is not a question of memories of nature but of memories of actuality.[1] This distinction is of the most far-reaching significance for the whole Gothic problem. For the actual is by no means identical with the natural. The actual can be quite clearly grasped, but that does not necessarily bring one nearer to nature. We rather discern the natural within the actual only when the idea of the organic has awakened within us, thereby endowing us with the capacity for active perceptive inspection. It is only then that, for us, the chaos of the actual merges into the cosmos of the natural. The conception of organic law can, however, only become vital when, as in the Classical epoch, an ideal relation of identity between man and the world is attained. The clarification of the world picture automatically follows from this relationship, for it is the transference of feeling (empathy) resulting from the consciousness of identity, which transforms all the inarticulate sounds of actuality into fixed, organically clear word forms.

Northern man was still far removed from this ideal consciousness of identity with the world. Consequently the natural world was still closed to him. But actuality pressed upon him all the more intensely. It yielded itself to him in all acuteness with its thousand details and accidents, because he observed it naively, unaided by any knowledge of the natural. It is this acuteness in the comprehension of actuality which differentiates Northern from Classical culture: the latter, avoiding the arbitrariness of actuality, builds itself up entirely on nature and her inner orderliness, thus enabling its organically rhythmed line-speech to pass over spontaneously into a direct representation of the natural.

Northern art, on the other hand, was evolved from the conjunction of an abstract linear speech with the reproduction of actuality. The first stage of this conjunction is exhibited in the Northern animal ornament. The specific expression of the line and its spiritual, non-sensuous mode of expression were in no way weakened by this interpolation of motives from actuality, for the natural, the organic, was still completely concealed in this actuality; and only the admission of such *organic* values of expression could have weakened the abstract character of the drawing.

[1] *Wirklichkeit*: "Actuality" seems preferable to "reality" as a translation of this word, since "reality" has metaphysical implications which are not intended in this context. [ED.]

On the other hand, this abstract character of the line could readily be amalgamated with values of actuality; indeed, these motives of actuality could, as we have seen, be evolved, even involuntarily, from this abstract linear fantasy. For what is characteristic of any impression of actuality reaches us in a kind of linear " shorthand," of which the single lines. contain a summary expressive value far exceeding the function of the line as a mere indication of outline. Caricature is the clearest instance of this mutual transposition between the characteristic line of actuality and the independent line that seeks only its own specific expression. In this case the summary expressive force of the single line threatens constantly to turn into a mere arabesque, while, on the contrary, at the beginning of the development, the purely abstract play of line tended readily to assume the characteristics of actuality.

But this fortuitous character in the genesis of indications of actuality only applies to the initial stages of the development of Northern ornament. As the development progressed, Northern man, with a growing selfconsciousness of artistic capacity, felt like all peoples of progressive development an intuitive need to subjugate the appearances of the outer world artistically, that is to say, to separate them from the vast, fluctuating sequence of appearances and to stabilize them in perceptible form. The process of this artistic stabilization has been the same in every human epoch, namely, the translation of the objects belonging to the outer world which are to be portrayed into the vocabulary of the contemporary will to form. This vocabulary of the will to form must be established before the artistic control of objects in the outer world can be attempted. It is the *a priori* of artistic configuration. The sphere in which the *a priori* will to form was established is known to us: it lies in ornament. This determines the *a priori* will to form with paradigmatic purity; that is to say, it becomes the exact expression of the relations in which the humanity of the period stands towards the world. It is only after the grammar of artistic speech has thus been established, that man can begin to translate the objects of the outer world into this speech.

The *a priori* will to form in primitive man is represented by the expressionless geometrical line, that absolute value set at the directly opposite pole to all life. By this means the way to an artistic adjustment with the outer world is indicated: the object is translated into this language of an inanimate geometry; it is geometricized and its expression of vitality is thereby subjugated. For this total subjugation of all vital expression is the aim of the primitive man's art, to which he is forced by his absolutely dualistic relationship to the world.

The will to form of Classical man is manifested in the organic rhythmic line of his ornament: he approaches the objects of the outer world with this ornamental idiom. To him, artistic portrayal means the accurate reproduction of the organic expressive value of the object; it means the transference of the expressive value of his language of ornament to the object to be portrayed.

By analysing Northern ornament we have come to know the essential character of the Gothic will to form; in this fantasy of line, with its feverishly enhanced activity devoid of all organic moderation, we discovered the intense yearning to create a non-sensuous, or rather, a super-sensuous world of spiritual expression; for to Northern man, fettered as he was to a chaotic picture of actuality, the merging into such a world must have been an ecstatic liberation. His artistic adjustment to the world could, therefore, only aim at assimilating the objects of the outer world to his specific language of line, that is to say, at interpolating them into this activity intensified and increased to its highest point of expression. The outer world offered him only confused impressions of actuality. He grasped these impressions with all their details quite accurately: but their mere material imitation had not, so far, had any artistic significance for him, for it had not freed any one single impression of actuality from the universal fluctuating sequence of appearances; objective imitation first became art when these impressions of actuality were combined with intensified intellectual complexes of expression. Arguing from a different standpoint, Lamprecht interprets the real position as follows:

" There is a period when artistic perception has no means of expression at its disposal but ornament. But this was not because Germanic eyes were unable to understand the animal world with its infinitely varied forms and changing movements quite as well as our eyes. It is quite certain, however, that at that time men did not see things as ornament, that is to say, crudely. But whenever the eye was the means of communicating aesthetic comprehension, whenever it was called upon to assist the artist to reproduce nature artistically, its receptive and comprehensive powers proved to be so limited, that only an ornamental rendering was felt to be a really aesthetic representation of natural forms."

And thus we reach the specifically dual, or rather the hybrid, effect of the whole of Gothic art: on the one hand, the most acute direct comprehension of actuality, on the other hand, a super-actual, fantastic play of line, uncontrolled by any object, vitalized only by its own specific expression. The whole development of the Gothic art of representation is determined by this counterplay and interplay. Briefly the stages of this artistic adjustment of Northern man to actuality are as follows (but it should be remembered that it is always a question of actuality alone, for only at the Renaissance does *nature* enter into the orbit of Northern man's vision and knowledge, and the Renaissance therefore represents the turning-point of the specifically Northern development): At first we have absolute dualism between man and actuality; elements of actuality are completely merged in the super-actual play of line; they completely disappear within it. Here the force of the artistic will is at its strongest, and the subjection of actuality is most consistent. The stage of animal ornament has been reached.

In the course of intellectual development the initial rigorous dualism between man and actuality ebbs slowly away: whilst in art as well the actual begins to receive more emphasis than the non-actual elements, even though the latter still always preponderate. As the values of actuality become more clamant, their amalgamation with these intellectual elements of expression, which are foreign to actuality, becomes more marked, consequently the hybrid character of Gothic art is strongest at this stage. This stage is represented, on the one hand, by the statuary of Gothic cathedrals, on the other hand by the Gothic treatment of drapery.

The connection between the Gothic cathedral statuary and the earlier ornament is relatively close. As in the latter the animal forms are completely merged into an independent linear movement, so the statues are merged in an independent architectural movement, of the utmost power of expression. The spiritual expression demanded by Gothic man was only obtained for these forms by connecting them with a spiritual world of expression which was independent of them. Out of their setting both the ornamental animal forms and the cathedral statuary are lifeless,

64

senseless, and expressionless; their spiritual power of expression, that is to say, their value as Gothic art, derives only from their incorporation into the abstract drawing and the abstract construction respectively, the expressive value of which is thus transferred to them. For the psychologist of style, the difference between animal ornament and cathedral statuary is merely qualitative, and easily explained in terms of progressive development; vague indications of animal forms have become statues with sharply accentuated physiognomies; confused drawing has become accurate construction.

The Gothic treatment of drapery shows us the stage where the factors of actuality counterbalance the elements of non-actuality: both are now equally developed but remain disconnected, unreconciled, in undisguised hybridism. For the counterplay of body and drapery, which is so characteristic of Middle Gothic art, is nothing but the counterplay of actuality and non-actuality, that is to say, super-reality. It is true, as a matter of fact, that we can only speak really of a counterplay of face and drapery, for in these representations it is not the body which comes into contrast with the drapery: the conception of actuality is concentrated in all its intensity in the naturalistic treatment of the face. And with this superb naturalism, so faithful to actuality, is contrasted and counterbalanced the drapery which the Gothic artist made the focus of non-actuality, an artful chaos of violently agitated lines possessing an independent vitality and expressive power which in this connection are uncanny.

What is here associated irreconcilably, and to our modern eye unmeaningly, attains to an ideal reconciliation in the highest stage of Northern development—more especially in the graphic art of a Holbein and a Dürer. Here naturalism and spiritual expression are no longer opposed; they are brought into a connection which is no longer outward but inward. Although the spiritualizing intent has lost its great force, it has become so highly sublimated, has become so much a matter of inwardness, that it can identify itself with the spiritual expression springing from the representation, that is to say, from the object represented itself. This spiritual expressiveness, therefore, is no longer forced on actuality from without, but is produced by it. And so we attain to that blending of the reproduction of actuality with the abstract play of line for which, as we have previously said, we have to thank the capacity for graphic characterization of Holbein and Dürer; which, within the framework of the *visual* arts, represents the very highest point attainable within the presuppositions of Northern art, and which, in its perfection, is therefore without parallel in the entire history of art. The capacity for characterization in drawing is quite unthinkable without this preliminary history of practice in purely abstract line. This it was which first enabled the inherent expression of the line, its independent spiritual existence, to combine so happily with the subservient function of the line when dependent on the object, that the spiritual expressive value of the line became simultaneously the interpreter of the spiritual energy of the thing represented. At this stage the mere juxtaposition of spiritual expression and reproduction of actuality becomes a co-operation which produced the highest capacity for spiritual characterization known in the history of art. In this concentrated representation of *spiritual* energies Gothic reaches its climax, the Northern art of abstract line reaches its climax, and the contrast between Gothic and Classical cannot be better emphasized than by bringing forward Michael Angelo for comparison, in whom to a certain extent the Classical, that is to say, the organically fettered art of expression, reached its zenith: the powerful representation of sensuous energies is here confronted with the most powerful representation of spiritual energies. Thus reverberates the contrast between Classical and Gothic. And here we can only indicate that after the admittance of irreconcilable Classical elements, such as were contributed by the European Renaissance, Northern art, deprived of all definite orientation, in general shows no longer the form, but only the content of the spiritual expressiveness demanded by its entire organization, which has, however, now been robbed of its necessary exponent, the abstract line. Indeed, the separation between form and content, known to no autochthonous art, was actually first introduced into Northern art by this general artistic disorientation. The tendency of Northern art to allegorical references, to literary significance, is the last offshoot of that yearning for spiritual expression which, robbed of its possibilities of natural formal embodiment by the dominance of an alien world of form, is now so superficially and inartistically grafted on to the work of art. The strongest Northern painters after the Renaissance were disguised men of letters, disguised poets, and to that extent those people who look upon the essence of

66

German art as inseparable from this literary note are, unhappily, not so very far wrong. The catastrophe of the Northern Renaissance is thereby only placed in a clearer light and thereby at the same time those people are justified who have turned from an art which has lost its ideal unity and sought connections where the artistic will still knows how to express itself in a purely formal manner. And in modern Europe, this is still perhaps only the case in France, where, indeed, in its modern art a kind of synthesis between Northern spirituality and Southern sensuousness has been achieved.

X

TRANSCENDENTALISM
OF THE GOTHIC WORLD OF EXPRESSION

We have said that the *a priori* will to form of any period of human history was always the adequate expression of its relations to the surrounding world. From the character of the Gothic will to form, as we have learned to know it in its most elementary but most striking form by analysing Northern ornament, we must therefore draw our understanding of the relations between Northern man and the outer world.

For guidance we have recourse again to the great specimen types in the history of mankind, as they have been established in previous chapters. In them the orderly connection between the will to form and world-feeling was perfectly clear. We saw that, in primitive man, who was still intellectually undeveloped, there was an absolute dualism, an unalleviated relationship of fear towards the phenomenal world, which in matters of art manifested itself naturally in the need for deliverance from the arbitrariness of the phenomenal world and a clinging to self-created values of an inevitable and absolute character. His art therefore was rooted in the need for deliverance: it was this need which imparted to it its transcendental character.

Oriental art, which also arises from the need for deliverance, exhibits the same transcendental character. As we have seen, the difference between the two is not one of kind, but only one of degree with regard to quality, such as is implied in the difference between primitiveness and culture. The similarity in kind of the psychical presuppositions is manifested in spite of all qualitative differences by the fact that, in both, the will to form is bound to the abstract, organically unsoftened line. Where the abstract line is the exponent of the will to form, art is transcendental, is conditioned by the need for deliverance. On the other hand, the organically determined line shows that this need of deliverance in a wide sense has gradually decreased and has been moderated to a merely individual need for deliverance, such as is, after all, proved in any tendency towards orderliness and harmony. Art is then no longer transcendental in the fullest meaning of the word.

As regards our Gothic problem, it would appear that this decrease and mitigation cannot yet have occurred; for the need of deliverance as a psychical presupposition of Gothic art has already been indicated by the fact that in it the abstract, organically unsoftened line is the vehicle of the will to form. On the other hand, we see that this need for deliverance is very plainly distinguished from that of primitive and Oriental man, for whereas primitive and Oriental man carry the artistic expression of their craving for deliverance to the utmost limits and are only able to rid themselves of the harassing arbitrariness of-the living, phenomenal world by the contemplation of inanimate, expressionless values, we see that the Gothic line is full of expression, full of vitality. In contrast with Oriental fatalism and quietism we have here a questing, impulsive movement, a restless activity. The dualistic relation towards the external world cannot therefore be present so strongly as in primitive and Oriental man. On the other hand, it cannot have been weakened by knowledge so much as it was in classical man, for then the line which has been purified in the organic sense would show the overcoming of all dualistic embarrassments.

Gothic line being essentially abstract, and yet at the same time strongly vital, shows us that a differentiated intermediate state exists, in which the dualism is no longer sufficiently strong to seek artistic freedom in the absolute negation of life, but is on the other hand not yet so weakened as to derive the meaning of art from the organic orderliness of life itself. Therefore the Gothic will to form exhibits neither the restfulness of expression due to absolute lack of knowledge, as does that of primitive man, nor the restfulness due to the absolute renunciation of knowledge, as does that of oriental man, nor yet the restfulness of stabilized belief in knowledge as it is demonstrated in the organic harmony of classical art. Its essential nature seems to be far more that of a restless urge which in its quest for rest, its seeking for deliverance, can find no satisfaction but that of stupefaction, of intoxication. And thus the dualism, which no longer suffices for the negation of life, which is already enfeebled by knowledge which nevertheless denies to it complete emancipation, resolves itself into a confused mania of ecstasy, a convulsive yearning to be merged

70

19. Church of St. Quirinus, Neuss

20.   Rheims Cathedral

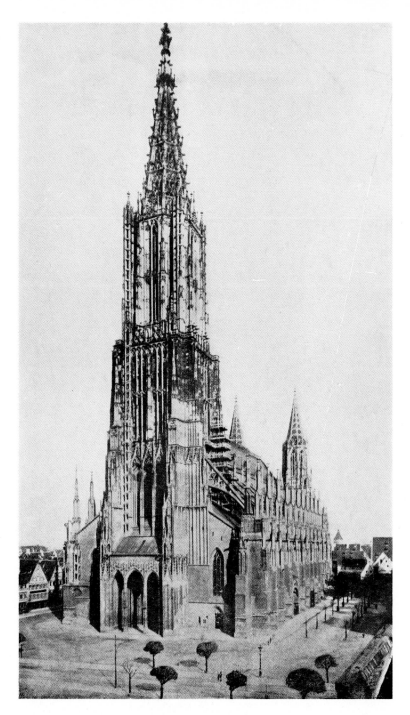

21. Ulm Cathedral

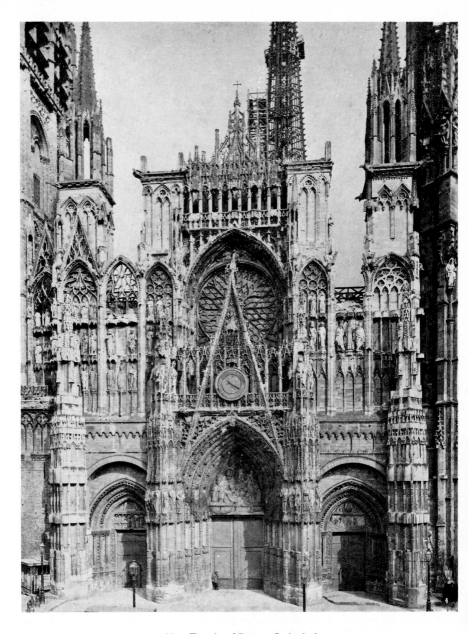

22. Façade of Rouen Cathedral

23.　Upper part of main doorway of Rheims Cathedral
Coronation of the Virgin

24. Flying buttresses, Cologne Cathedral

25. Ruins of the Abbey of Jumièges
(*photo: Gérard Franceschi, Aulnay-sous-Bois*)

26.   Nave of Cologne Cathedral

into a super-sensuous rapture, into a pathos, the specific essence of which is a lack of all measure.

In Northern ornament, then, the Gothic soul is already clearly reflected: it is the graph of its sensibility which the line now describes. The unsatisfied impulse existing in this confusion of lines, clutching greedily at every new intensification, to lose itself finally in the infinite, is its impulse, its life. It has lost the innocence of lack of knowledge, but has, as yet, been unable to win its way, either to the oriental's superb renunciation of knowledge, or to classical man's happiness in knowledge; and therefore, bereft of all pure, natural satisfaction, it can only wear itself out in a convulsive, unnatural satisfaction. But this violent exaltation sweeps it into spheres of sensibility, in which it finally loses its feeling of inward discord, in which it finds emancipation from its restless, confused relation towards the image of the external world. Distressed by actuality, debarred from naturalness, it aspires to a world above the actual, above the sensuous. It uses this tumult of sensations to lift itself out of itself. It is only in intoxication that it experiences the thrill of eternity. It is this exalted hysteria which is above all else the distinguishing mark of the Gothic phenomenon.

The same convulsed feeling expressed by Northern ornament in the pathos of its linear fantasy gives rise later to the non-sensuous, super-sensuous pathos of Gothic architecture. Northern ornament leads in a direct line to Gothic architecture. The will to form which, at first, could only express itself on the free, material, unconfined field of ornamental activity, gradually increased so much in strength that it finally succeeded in subjugating the rigid, unyielding material of architecture for its own purposes and, goaded to the highest productive power by natural resistance, found in it precisely its most imposing expression.

This pathetic note can be recognized also in other spheres as the basic element of the Northern will to form. The very peculiar interlacing of words and sentences in early Northern poetry, its artful chaos of interrelated ideas, the expressive rhythm imposed upon it by alliteration and the intricate repetition of the initial sounds (corresponding to the repetition of motives in ornament and producing in the same way the character of a confused, unending melody): all these are unmistakable analogies to Northern ornament. Germanic poetry does not know how to express rest or equipoise; it is all movement. " Germanic poetry knows no contemplative absorption into a peaceful condition: its poetry dreams of no actionless idyll: its attention is concentrated on stirring action and the flood tide of emotion. . . . Our ancestors must have been specially influenced by the feeling of pathos, otherwise the fashioning of this poetry cannot be the faithful expression of their inner mood " (Lamprecht).

What has already been betrayed by the character of Northern ornament is thus confirmed. Where the enhanced pathetic note dominates, there is an inward dissonance to be overcome: all pathos is foreign to a healthy soul. It is only when the soul is denied its natural outlets, when it has not yet found its equilibrium, that its inward oppression remains at such unnatural tension. Here it is only necessary to think of the exaggerated pathos of the period of puberty when, under the pressure of critical inner adjustments, ecstatic spiritual longings manifest themselves in such uncontrolled fashion. " So much, however, is certain, that the vague, expansive feelings of youth and of uncivilized peoples are alone adapted to the *sublime*, which, whenever it has to be awakened in us by external objects, must be evolved from *shapeless* or *intangible* forms, and must surround us with a greatness to which we have not yet attained. . . . But just as the sublime is so easily engendered by twilight and night, when shapes are easily confused, so by daylight, which divides and defines all things, it is dispelled, and thus by every developing image it will be undone." These words of Goethe's might serve as a motto for the whole of our observations.

Thus the paradigm afforded by ornament tells us enough about the discord which determined the Gothic will to form. Where unison reigns between man and the outer world, where an inner point of balance has been found, as with classical man, there the will to form comports itself as a will to harmony, as a will to equilibrium, as a will towards organic compactness. There it constructs those happy and satisfying forms, which correspond to the security of knowledge and the inward joy of existence which results from it. Deterred by no obstacles, untouched by any longing for transcendency, it lives out its life serenely within the bonds of human organic being. A glance at Greek ornament confirms this statement.

But this unison was lacking in the Gothic soul. For it, the inner world and the outer world are still unreconciled and the unreconciled opposites strive for redemption in transcendental spheres, in intensified psychical conditions. A final liberation must therefore—and this is the determining factor—still be considered possible, the consciousness of an uncompromising dualism must still be lacking. The opposites are not considered as irreconcilable, but only as not yet reconciled. And the difference between the expressionless, abstract line of Oriental man and the intensified expression of the abstract line of Gothic man is just the difference between a final definitive dualism, born of a most profound insight into the world, and a provisional dualism of a still undeveloped stage of knowledge; that is to say, the difference between the sublime quietism of old age and the exalted pathos of youth.

The dualism of Gothic man is not superior to knowledge, as in oriental man, but prior to knowledge. It consists partly of a vague presentiment, partly of a bitter experience of facts. His dualistic sufferings have not yet been transformed into reverence. He still strives against dualistic inevitableness and endeavours to overcome it by an unnatural enhancement of sensibility. The feeling of dualistic distraction, which is neither overcome by rational, sensuous knowledge in the Classical sense, nor softened and enlightened by profound metaphysical insight as in the Oriental fashion, leaves him neither rest nor peace. He feels himself enslaved by higher powers, which he merely fears without worshipping. With his joyless fear of the world, he stands as a product of earthly unrest and metaphysical anxiety, midway between the all-embracing piety of the Greek, a piety organically developed from rationalism and naive sensuousness, and the Oriental's renunciation of the world, which he has refined into a religion. And as rest and clear vision are denied him, his only resource is to increase his restlessness and confusion to the pitch where they bring him stupefaction and release.

The need in Northern man for activity, which is precluded from being translated into a clear knowledge of actuality and which is intensified for lack of this natural solution, finally disburdens itself in an unhealthy play of fantasy. Actuality, which Gothic man could not transform into naturalness by means of clear-sighted knowledge, was overpowered by this intensified play of fantasy and transformed into a spectrally heightened and distorted actuality. Everything becomes weird and fantastic.

Behind the visible appearance of a thing lurks its caricature, behind the lifelessness of a thing an uncanny, ghostly life, and so all actual things become grotesque. His impulse towards knowledge, being denied its natural satisfaction, thus exhausts itself in wild fantasies. And just as an underlying current links the chaotic play of line in Northern ornament to the refined constructive art of Gothic architecture, so in the same way the wild fantasies of this spiritual immaturity are linked to the refined construction of scholasticism. Common to all is an urge to activity, which, being bound to no one object, loses itself, as a result, in infinity. In the ornament and in the early life of fantasy, we can only discern chaos; in Gothic architecture and in scholasticism, this crude chaos has grown into an artful and refined chaos. The will to form remains the same throughout the entire development, only it passes through all the stages from utmost primitiveness to utmost culture.

XI

NORTHERN RELIGIOUS FEELING

However little is known of the religious feeling of Northern man before his acceptance of Christianity, however much tradition fails us on this point, the general nature of this feeling can nevertheless be indicated. A condition of fantastic fear inclining towards religiosity, accompanied by a vague differentiation, indeed by a fusion of the actual and the non-actual seems here to have been the decisive factor. So, between the beautiful, clear-cut, plastic character of the Classical Olympus and the quite unplastic, impersonal transcendentalism of the Orient, there comes this hybrid world of Northern gods and spirits. Just when this world of gods appears to be within one's grasp, it eludes one to melt into formless phantoms, and between the formed and the formless there seems to be no transition, no border line. " The figures of the gods have something intangible about them; every time they were personified the nature of their powers appeared to elude the application of any human standard. This seems to be the reason why the Germanic gods seem such formless figures, without any constant limits to their functions. As a general rule the chief gods, at any rate, were considered as impersonal, in the mysterious gloom of the forests " (Lamprecht).

In the crude eudemonism of its general ideas, Northern religiosity differs but little from other nature religions. But behind this eudemonism, though it claims first attention, the searching eye at once discovers the strong substratum of imaginative fear, which, rising from dualistic unrest, peoples the Northern world of gods with ghosts, spectres, and spooks. An urge to body forth fantastic shapes is here at work, creating from the play of impressions a play of wild, confused spirits, who now and then assume a shape only to dissolve into formlessness upon nearer investigation. A certain instability, a certain restless activity is common to this entire world of spirits and ghosts. Northern man knows nothing of repose; his entire power of configuration concentrates itself on the representation of uncontrolled, boundless agitation. The storm spirits are his nearest kin.

Our information as to the religious cult also is very fragmentary. It was far removed from devotional reverence and submission to the deity: the cult exhausted itself in fear-laden incantations and a wealth of sacrifices for the appeasement of wayward, supernatural powers.

The difference between the Northern spirit world and the classical world of gods gives us the best clue to the peculiarity of Germanic religious feeling. On the one hand we have a vague impersonal agitation, a tremendous force as it were of abstract energies, which takes shape only occasionally and then in a deceptive, enigmatic, irritating manner (just as the tremendous force of the abstract line in ornament is shot through with indications of actuality); and on the other hand, we have a quiescent, corporeally comprehensible, clear plasticity, free from deception and enigma. But not even Greek humanity reached this perfection of organic creative power all at once; it, too, had to overcome old dualistic anxieties, partly composed of rudiments of crude stages of development and partly due to contamination with oriental spiritualism, though the Greek Homer, with his belief in gods, already stands in the full light of day and all misty spectres and ghosts have disappeared. The development from the vague fear of ghosts, from a gloomy, turbid fatalism to a cosmic conception of the universe and a corresponding plastic conception of the world of gods, is described by Erwin Rohde in his *Psyche* as follows: " To the depths of his being the Greek, Homer, is conscious of his limitations, his dependence upon the powers which rule around him. Gods rule over him with a magic sway, unwisely it may frequently seem, but the idea has been awakened of a general, universal order, a fitting together, according to their allotted parts ($\mu o \tilde{\iota} \rho \alpha$) of the interlacing events of life, of the individual and of the community; the wilfulness of each particular daemon is curtailed. A belief is heralded that the world is a cosmos, a well-conceived ordinance such as the governments of men seek to establish. A belief in wild, spectral doings could not flourish side by side with such conceptions. Such spectral doings, as distinct from the actions of the real gods, are always to be recognized by the fact that they stand outside the general scheme of coherent activity, that they give free play to all the evil desires of the various invisible powers. The irrational, the unaccountable is the essence of the belief in spirits and ghosts: herein lies the peculiar horror of this domain of belief or delusion, and herein also lies the unstable vacillation of its forms. Homeric religion is already rationalized, its gods are perfectly comprehensible to the Greek mind, perfectly plain and clearly perceptible in form and bearing to the Greek imagination."

This is an unvarnished statement—which will serve as an important side-light for our Gothic problem—that the beautiful creation of the Greek world of gods does not exclude, as might have been imagined, a rationalistic conception of the world, but is directly completed by it, as the other side of an anthropocentric, anthropomorphic power of configuration, which draws its energies from the felicitous feeling of unity with the outer world.

Unhappily, no Rohde has yet been found to write a Northern " Psyche " for us. As we have said, on that point we are groping almost completely in the dark, for the available material is altogether scanty; moreover, it is distorted by later additions of a Christian tendency. Nevertheless, the meagre information we possess as to the religious views of Northern man confirm for us, as we have seen, what early art revealed to us concerning the hybrid character of its psychical make-up. Northern mythology of the more mature periods can only be adduced with the utmost caution for the interpretation of Northern religious feeling, its connection with actual religious sensibility being very loose. It has more to do with the history of literature than with the history of religion.

Direct interpretation, however, does not give us the fullest information as to the psychical make-up of Northern man: better results are obtained from conclusions which can quite safely be drawn from the later stages of development, of which better accounts have come down to us. And the most fruitful event in this connection is the Northern acceptance of Christianity. A nation will accept no religion which is utterly and entirely alien to its nature, even if it is forcibly imposed. Certain favourable responsive conditions must be to hand. When the ground is not in some way prepared beforehand, a strong and brutal power may obtain an outward, superficial acceptance, but will never compel the roots to strike deeper. And Christianity struck root, not merely in the superficial strata but in the deeper substrata of Northern feeling, even if it did not succeed in reaching *all* the strata. Certain spiritual conditions must therefore have paved the way for its reception. All the mythological polytheism had been unable to destroy a certain fatalistic disposition, monotheistic in its tendency, which existed in the composition of the Northern mind. Indeed, this disposition grew more pronounced and finally led to a " Twilight of the Gods," to the downfall of the old polytheistic, spectral conception of the gods: and in their stead was born the gloomy, inexorable, fateful power of the Norns. The development thus pressed on towards monotheism and, as Christianity with its worship of saints and martyrs presented a certain substitute for those polytheistic needs which had not, as yet, been completely suppressed, the exchange of mythological for Christian ideas was well prepared for.

For the North, Christianity's greatest persuasive power lay in its systematic structure. It was the completeness of the Christian system which conquered the unsystematic Northern man with his chaotic, nebulous mysticism.

Northern man lacked the requisite energy for the independent construction of a fixed form for his transcendental needs. His spiritual powers were consumed by inward strife and therefore never attained to any unified achievement. The desire for action gave out with the fatigue of overcoming so many obstacles, and what remained was only a melancholy feeling of impotence which longed for the bewilderment of intoxication. Until he had attained inner maturity this consciousness of weakness made Northern man powerless to resist any complete system imposed upon him from without, whether it was Roman law or Christianity. And when, as in Christianity, chords vibrated in unison with his own distraught nature, when his uncertain, nebulous, transcendental ideas were met by a wonderfully constructed and logical system of a cognate, transcendental character, this system was bound to have a convincing effect on him, overriding and suppressing any slight resistance. The longing to come to rest in a fixed form could not but overcome any discrepancies between his own and the alien ideas: the subject-matter, content, and secondary features of his own ideas were subordinated to the alien concepts and then adapted to the new form more rapidly than could have been believed of the dull Northerner. Nevertheless, the Christian system always remained merely a substitute for the form which Northern

86

man could not previously create by his own energy. There could therefore be no question of an absolutely complete absorption into Christianity, and when the North, tempted by the form ready to hand, had succumbed to it, many parts of its being remained excluded from this form which it had not itself created. To find an appropriate form for his dualistic hybrid nature, to systematize his chaotic yearning for ecstasy, this was reserved for the highest point in the development of Northern man, the mature Gothic. Christian scholasticism, and in a far higher degree Gothic architecture, these only were the proper realizations of this Northern will to form, which was so hard to satisfy; and to these therefore we shall give attention in detail. For the present we may be satisfied with finding the fact of his acceptance of Christianity confirming our verdict on the character of Northern man, reached solely by way of the psychological analysis of the style manifested in his earliest artistic efforts. For this enabled us to know the nature of the will to form which is adequate for his relationship to the outer world, and which consequently determines all the manifestations of his life.

XII

THE PRINCIPLE
OF CLASSICAL ARCHITECTURE

Every age is strongly biased in favour of the artistic activity which corresponds most nearly to its particular will to form; preference is given to the art or the technique whose particular means of expression offers the best guarantee that this will to form will be given free and unhindered expression. Therefore, when we investigate the historical facts and seek to discover which are the predominant types of art in the various epochs, we have already found the most important and most fundamental method for determining the will to form of the period under discussion. And by this means we attain the only really correct point of view from which we can approach the interpretation of the stylistic factors concerned. When, for example, we know that in the Classical period, sculpture, and more especially the plastic representation of ideal human beauty, was predominant, we have already discovered the *Leitmotiv*, the fundamental principle of Greek art; we have found immediately the key which will reveal to us the inmost being of all other types of Greek art. The Greek temple, for instance, cannot be understood by itself: it is only when we have recognized in Greek sculpture the fundamental principle of Greek artistic creation in its paradigmatic purity, that we shall understand the Greek temple and be able to realize how the Greek with purely static, purely constructive conditions attempted to express, and succeeded in expressing, those laws of the beauty of organic being for which at the zenith of his art he found the most direct and clearest expression in a literal, plastic representation of beautiful human beings. And in similar fashion the types of art of the Italian Renaissance will first become comprehensible to us in their development only when we have heard and understood the last and clearest word, uttered by Raphael, concerning them.

Thus, every manifestation of style has its climax, in which the will to form in question is found as though it were an isolated " culture." If, in the presence of Gothic, we consider in which form of artistic expression, that is to say, in which artistic technique, it best attained its aims, there can be no doubt as to the reply. We need only utter the word Gothic to awaken in us immediately the powerfully associated idea of Gothic architecture. This inevitable connection of ideas between Gothic and architecture coincides with the historical fact, that the stylistic epoch of Gothic was completely dominated by architecture, that all other artistic manifestations were either directly dependent upon it or, at any rate, played a secondary part in comparison with it.

When we speak of antique classical art, the first idea which arises in us is that of antique sculpture with the names of its masters: if we speak of Italian art the names of Masaccio, Leonardo, Raphael, and Titian are the first on our lips; but when we speak of Gothic, the image of a Gothic cathedral immediately rises before us. And the inner connection between Gothic and Baroque, which has already been indicated, conforms to the fact that the first idea evoked in 'connection with the latter is also that of architecture.

The term Gothic is therefore inseparable from the image of Gothic cathedrals: all the crowding energies of the will to form attain their apotheosis, their brilliant climax in Gothic architecture. And we may say here at once, that the Gothic will to form exhausted itself and ran itself to death in this, the highest production of its energy: thus alone can we explain its inability to resist the invasion of alien ideals of art at the Renaissance.

The absolute predominance of architecture in Gothic art confirms what the analysis of Northern ornament has revealed to us concerning the nature of the Gothic will to form. For, since the language of architecture is abstract, since the laws of its construction are distinct from all organic laws, being rather of an abstract, mechanical nature, so in the Gothic tendency to self-expression in architecture we observe merely a parallel to ornament, which, as we have seen, is dominated by its inherent expression (that is to say, by the mechanical expressive value of the line) and is consequently likewise dominated by abstract values.

Ornament and architecture therefore play the decisive part in Gothic. They alone by the nature of their means of expression can offer an artistic manifestation adequate for the will to form. In sculpture, painting, and drawing there is from the first a certain danger for the unalloyed expression of the will to form: indeed, they contain inward starting points for the realization of the Classical will to form, which clearly demonstrate how from here onwards the authority of the Renaissance gained ground and dispossessed the old will to form.

The tendencies to expression which had been so peculiarly modified by the play of abstract lines in ornament were bound to remain valid for Gothic architecture as well. An investigation of the character of Gothic architecture will support this statement. And for an antithetical example we will hold closely to Classical architecture, for it provides us with an antithetical appearance of a will to form which, from its very nature, was compelled to express itself organically, not abstractly, overcoming the abstract quality of the architectural means of expression.

For the architectonic world is vast, and the possibilities for the expression of architectural laws are as wide and unlimited as the laws themselves and their means of expression are limited. It is true that the laws of all architecture are the same, but not the expression in architecture attained by the application of these laws. In this sense, architectural desire for expression is quite as independent as any other of the arts specially designated as " free." And the history of architecture is made up precisely of the transformation into ever fresh forms of expression, under pressure of the changing will to form, of the comparatively meagre store of constructional types. The history of architecture is not a history of technical developments but the history of changing expressive aims and of the ways and means whereby technique is adapted and made serviceable to these changing aims by ever new and different combinations of its basic elements. It is no more a history of technique than the history of philosophy is a history of logic. And here too we see how logic, how the few basic types of thinking, are ever transformed into new formulations of thought, adequate to the state of mind concerned.

To sharpen our eye for understanding the possibilities of architectural expression, we will begin by investigating the principle of Classical building. This is all the more accessible to us because in architectonics, as in every other sphere, we are dependent upon the antique Classical traditions revived by the European Renaissance. At the present day it is also easier to read a Greek philosopher than a mediaeval scholastic philosopher.

If we seek for the architectural member most peculiar to Classical architecture, the column immediately presents itself for our consideration. What determines the impression made by the column is its roundness. This roundness at once evokes the illusion of organic vitality, because it directly reminds us of the roundness of those natural limbs which exercise a similar function of support, and more especially of the tree-trunk, which supports the crown, and of the flower-stalk which bears the flower. Besides which, roundness in itself satisfies our natural organic feeling without the need of evoking analogous ideas. We cannot look at anything round without inwardly realizing the process which created that roundness. We seem, as it were, to realize the certainty, devoid of all violence, with which the centripetal forces concentrated in the centre, that is to say, the axis of the pillar, hold the centrifugal forces in check and steady them; we are conscious of the drama of this happy balance, we feel the self-sufficiency of the column, the eternal melody which throbs within its roundness, we feel above all the calm which evolves from this perpetual self-contained movement. Thus the column, like the circle, is the highest symbol of self-contained and perfected organic life.

But these are feelings awakened by the column as a single member, quite apart from its structural function. These feelings are intensified when we consider the column as a member in a structural organism. The structural function of the column is naturally that of support. This function would naturally be equally well performed by a rectangular supporting member. Therefore, tectonically, the round column is not necessary. But surely it is artistically necessary, that is to say, in the sense of the Classical idea of form. For to it falls the task of *expressing* the function of bearing, of making it perceptible, that is to say, making it directly comprehensible to our organically determined feeling. To this organic faculty for visualization, the rectangular column would be an inanimate mass utterly impenetrable to our feeling for vitality, to our organic power of imagination. But this imaginative power is at once awakened by the round column, experiencing the drama of forces of which this bearing and supporting member is the scene. The preponderance of vertical extension over extension in width is already decisive. If we wish to interpret this difference in dimension in an organic sense, we may say that the activity of the coalescence is subordinate to the activity of the self-lifting effort. We feel how the column draws itself together, concentrates all its forces from all sides on to the axis in order to exert with all its force the vertical uplifting energy condensed in the axis; in short, we feel how it carries. There can be no clearer, more convincing, more satisfying expression of assured, effortless support than that presented by the column. With a rectangular support we should only be able to assert that it was supporting, because the result would convince us of the fact; but in this case, we feel it, we believe it, here it has an aspect of necessity, because it is imposed upon our organic imagination.

To this must be added the emphasizing of the vertical tendency by grooving or fluting. One need only imagine this fluting following the column round horizontally at once to perceive that it would convey an impression of collapse, of yielding beneath the burden, instead of an impression of easy self-lifting. The passive function of burden would then be more strongly emphasized than the active function of support, and the expression of freedom in the adjustment between burden and energy would be impeded.

We see, therefore, that the Greek will to form, which represents the harmonious Classical consciousness of unity between man and the outer world and which consequently culminates in the representation of organic life, is also expended in the endeavour to transform all tectonic necessity into organic necessity. This endeavour is most strikingly manifest in the general plan of the Greek temple, more especially in the relation between the *cella* and peristyle. In this, we have a striking example of the independence of constructive idea and constructive aim, and of the great superiority of the former to the latter. The practical aim of Greek construction was merely to provide the statue of the divinity with an enclosed space, safe from all the inclemencies of the weather. But this purpose of space creation could not be turned to aesthetic account, because the Greek had no artistic relation to space. The Greek disposition was rather plastic in its direction, not in a literal, but in a metaphorical sense, that is to say, the whole of Greek thought, feeling, and experience was directed towards compact, clearly defined corporeality, towards a stable, compact, substantial being. In this manner he had transformed the entire incomprehensibility of the world into clear comprehensibility. Greek gods, Greek thought, Greek art, all have the same immediately comprehensible plastic quality. Everything immaterial is ruled out and the real immateriality is space. Space is something spiritual, intangible, and it was only when the Greek mind lost its naive, sure, plastic quality by contact with the Orient in Hellenistic times that Greek tectonics, which was independent of space, became an architecture creative of space.

The creation of the *cella* could not therefore satisfy the Greek will to form: the constructive principle found no support in the structural purpose. To transform practical requirements into artistic requirements, a great deviation was necessary. To the structural nucleus demanded by the practical purpose of the building, there was given, by means of the peristyle, an envelope entirely free from any practical purpose, a dress which need serve no purpose other than the aesthetic fitness adequate to Greek feeling. The structural nucleus, as such, falls aesthetically into the background; what stands out is only the tectonic, external framework in its clear, rhythmic, comprehensible, plastic quality. A work of art is thus evolved from a merely utilitarian building.

The fundamental procedure of all pure tectonics is the adjustment of the burdening beams to the carrying supports. This adjustment, which is really quite abrupt, almost catastrophic, is made organically clear and smooth by the Greek constructive sense, is transformed into a perfect and pleasing spectacle of living forces by the system of columns and architrave, which inspires us with a feeling of inward well-being. The rigid logic of construction is transformed into a living organism, the strict counterpoint of architectonic laws which have no relation to life becomes a harmonious rhythm corresponding to the inner rhythm of Greeksensibility.

The tendency to modify in an organic sense the adjustment between burden and power, which is always an adjustment between vertical and horizontal tendencies, is no doubt expressed in the creation of the pediment. The pediment also has no direct practical necessity, merely an aesthetic one. Its aesthetic function is to find a termination satisfactory to organic feeling for the hard clash, inevitable for reasons of statics, between the horizontal and the vertical systems.

93

What the pediment accomplishes on a large scale is achieved on a small one by the structural members intervening between the burdening beams and the carrying supports, more especially by the capitals of the pillars. The organically disciplined feeling longs for a mitigation of the shock between burden and power, an organic reconciliation of the mechanically unreconciled, and it is precisely the capital which undertakes this task of reconciliation and mitigation. It takes away the catastrophe of the shock, by preparing for it and allowing it to die away. In this connection, to investigate the organically interpretative force of the details of the Greek system of columns and architrave would take us too long. Nevertheless, we will at least point out the difference between the Ionic and the Doric styles, because we have already come across it in the sphere of ornament and it has shown us that in Greece, the Doric element provided the connecting link between Mediterranean culture and the North. It is characteristic that the organic refinement of constructive processes has not gone so very far in the Doric temple. A certain masculine clumsiness, a certain masculine reserve, prevented the Doric mind from emancipating itself too entirely from the constructive constraint of architecture. It still strives for a sublimity which is organically quite inexpressible, and can only become effective in abstract language. Its Northern origin is betrayed by this longing for a superhuman, supersensuous pathos. Taine laconically remarks of the Doric style: " Trois ou quatre formes élémentaires de la géometrie font tous les frais."

In the Doric style, as a consequence of this pathos, the burdening forces are more prominent than the supporting ones. The weight of the burden was so great that the supporting columns were forced to become wider: they swell out towards the base, thereby diverting to the foundations of the building the pressure which they themselves are unable to sustain. Thus they do not die away within themselves, as do Ionic columns, which are clearly separated from the general foundation by a definitive base, but they as it were die into the ground.

The structural limitations of the Doric temple and the consequent compression of its general proportions certainly make it ponderous, but they also give it its unequalled solemnity and majestic aloofness. In the Ionic style everything is lighter, more flowing, more vital, more supple, more humanly approachable. What is lost in structural gravity

27.   Detail of Church of St. Lawrence, Nuremberg,
with the spire of the Tabernacle by Adam Krafft

28. Vaulting of the Choir of the Liebfrauenkirche, Treves
(*photo: Preussischen Messbildanstalt, Berlin*)

29.   Interior of the Church of St. George, Dinkelsbühl
        (*photo: Dr. Franz Stoedtner, Düsseldorf*)

30.   The Great Refectory of the Castle of Marienburg

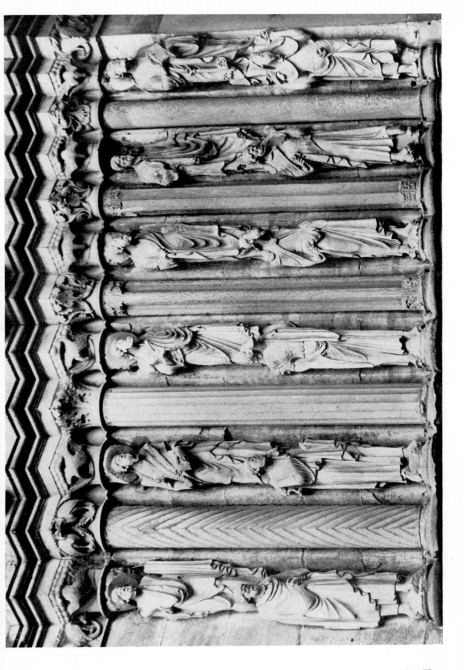

31. Prophets sup-
porting Apostles.
Bamberg Cathedral

32.   Cornice with Lion, and detail of the Resurrection.
Freiburg Cathedral, Saxony
(*photo: Dr. Franz Stoedter, Düsseldorf*)

33. Roof sculptures. Amiens Cathedral

34.　The Apostle Peter.　St. Pierre, Moissac

is gained in expressive cheerfulness. All restraint due to the demands of the material itself, that is to say, due to structural laws, has vanished: the stone is made completely sensuous, is replete with organic life, and all the restraints which constitute the power and grandeur of the Doric style are as it were playfully overridden. The Doric temple presents itself to us as a sublime drama, the Ionic as an exhilarating play of free energies.

XIII

THE PRINCIPLE
OF GOTHIC ARCHITECTURE

We may best pass to the investigation of the principle of Gothic architecture and of its characteristics—differing entirely from those of Greek
tectonics—by making clear the relation in which both building styles
stand to their material, stone. Architecture begins to be an art from the
moment that it ceases to be satisfied with employing stone as merely the
material for some practical aim or another, and with treating it according
to 'the strict nature of the material, but seeks to wrest from the lifeless
nature of the material an expression corresponding to a certain *a priori*
artistic will. We have seen that Greek art animated this lifeless nature
of stone, making it a wonderfully expressive organism (as in ornament it
animated the dead abstract line of primitive man into an organically
rounded and organically rhythmed line). From the rigid, non-sensuous
logic of construction it evolved a sensuously felt and sensuously comprehensible play of living forces. Between logical orderliness and organic
necessity, a synthesis is created which is entirely in accordance with the
other ideal classical syntheses of concept and intuition, of thought and
experience, of intelligence and sensibility. To ensure an ideal synthesis,
the component factors must be equal, they must interpenetrate, support,
and complete each other. And this of course means that this architectural
synthesis is not due to a forcible subjugation of the stone and its material
laws: rather the structural laws pass imperceptibly and without abrupt-
ness into organic laws. Thus Classical architecture attains its vital expressive value without in any way renouncing stone and its material laws.

To affirm stone means to express architectonically the adjustment of
weight and energy. For the essence of stone is weight and its architectonic suitability is based on the law of gravity. The primitive builder
used the weight of the stone only for practical purposes, the classical
builder employed it artistically as well: he expressly affirmed it by

making the adjustment of weight and energy the artistic principle of the building. He affirmed the stone by changing its structural laws into organic, vital laws, that is to say, by making it sensuous. All expression to which Greek architecture attained was attained *through* the stone, *by means of* the stone; all expression to which Gothic architecture attained, was attained—and this is the full significance of the contrast—*in spite of* the stone. Its expression was not derived from the material but from the negation of it, by means only of its dematerialization.

If we cast a glance at the Gothic cathedral, we see only a kind of petrified, vertical movement from which every law of gravity seems to be eliminated. We see only an enormously strong upward movement of energies in opposition to the natural downward weight of the stone. There are no walls, no mass, to procure for us an impression of fixed material existence, only a thousand separate energies speak to us, whose substantiality we are hardly conscious of, for they act only as vehicles of an immaterial expression, as bearers of an uncontrolled upward movement. Vainly we seek for that indication of the relation between weight and energy which our feelings demand: weight does not appear to exist; we see only free and uncontrolled energies striving heavenward with an enormous *élan*. It is evident that stone is here entirely released from its material weight, that it is only the vehicle of a non-sensuous, incorporeal expression, in short, here it has become dematerialized.

This Gothic dematerialization of stone in favour of a purely spiritual mode of expression answers to the de-geometrization of the abstract line, as we have seen it occur in ornament, in favour of the same purpose, that of expression.

Spirit is the opposite of matter. To dematerialize stone is to spiritualize it. And by this statement we have made clear that the tendency of Greek architecture towards sensuousness is in direct contrast to the tendency of Gothic architecture towards spiritualization.

The Greek architect approached his material, stone, with a certain sensuousness and therefore allowed the material to express itself as such. But the Gothic architect approached stone with a desire for purely spiritual expression, that is to say, with structural intentions conceived artistically and independently of stone, and for which stone was only the external and submissive means for realization. An abstract system of construction is the result, wherein the stone plays a merely practical and not an artistic part. The mechanical energies, which are as it were dormant in the massiveness of the stone, have been awakened by the Gothic struggle for expression; they have become autocratic and have so far consumed the bulk of the stone that the visible firmness of the material is replaced by merely calculable statics. In short, out of the stone as mass, with its weight, emerges a bare, constructional scaffolding of stone. Architecture, which was a mason's art, develops into a stone-cutter's art, into a non-sensuous, constructive art. The contrast between Classical building organism and Gothic building system becomes the contrast between a living, breathing body and a skeleton.

Greek architecture is applied construction, Gothic architecture is pure construction. The constructive element in the first case is merely the means to a practical end; in the latter case it is an end in itself, for it coincides with artistic intentions of expression. Because the Gothic will to expression was able to become articulate in the abstract speech of structural relations, construction was carried for its own sake far beyond its practical aim. In this sense, Gothic architecture might be described as an aimless mania for construction; for it has no direct object, no direct practical aim: it is merely subservient to the artistic will to expression. And we know what the aim of this Gothic will to expression is: it is the longing for absorption in a non-sensuous, mechanical activity of the highest potency. When, later on, we consider scholasticism, the phenomenon contemporaneous with Gothic architecture, we shall see how it also truly reflected the Gothic will to expression. Here too is an excess of constructive subtlety without any direct objective, that is to say, without any aim of knowledge—for knowledge has already been established by the revealed truths of church and dogma; here, too, an excess of constructive subtlety serves no object but that of creating an endless activity, continuously intensified, in which the spirit loses itself as if in ecstasy. In scholasticism, as in architecture, there is the same logical frenzy, the same methodical madness, the same rationalistic expenditure for an irrational aim; and if we recall now the confused chaos of Northern ornament, which was as it were an abstract, incorporeal rendering of an endless, aimless movement, we see how this first dull awakening of the impulse to artistic activity had merely prepared the way for that which, later on, was perfected with such high refinement in architecture and scholasticism. The homogeneity of the will to form throughout the course of many centuries is thus clearly revealed.

But it would be a cardinal error to consider scholasticism and Gothic architecture as merely logical cleverness. They are only such for those who do not discern the will to expression striving towards the transcendental, that will which lies at the back of this purely structural, purely logical system, employing these structural elements only as a means. For when we said previously that the structure in Gothic architecture was an end in itself, that was only true in so far as structure was the appropriate vehicle for the artistic will to expression. For mere observation will certainly not enable us to understand the constructive processes of Gothic. Such comprehension can only be attained indirectly, as it were by calculation and the help of the drawing-board. By mere observation we shall hardly become conscious of the structural significance of the individual members of a Gothic building: the isolated member will more likely impress the beholder as being merely a mimic exponent of abstract expression. The sum total of logical calculations is therefore not in the end put forward for its own sake, but for the sake of a superlogical effect. The resultant expression goes far beyond the means by which it was attained, and the sight of a Gothic cathedral does not impress our minds as being a display of structural processes but as an outburst of transcendental longing expressed in stone. A movement of superhuman force carries us up with it into the intoxication of an endless willing and craving: we lose the feeling of our earthly bonds, we merge into an infinite movement which annihilates all finite consciousness.

Every nation in its art creates ideal possibilities for the liberation of its sense of vitality. The sense of vitality of Gothic man is oppressed by a dualistic distraction and restlessness. To remove this oppression he needs a state of the highest possible excitement, of highest pathos. Gothic man raises his cathedral into the infinite, not from a playful delight in construction, but in order that the sight of this vertical movement, far surpassing all human standards, may liberate in him that tumult of sensation in which alone he can silence his inner discord, in which alone he can find bliss. The beauty of the finite was sufficient for the inward exaltation of Classical man; Gothic man, dualistically riven and therefore transcendentally disposed, could only feel the thrill of eternity in the infinite. The culmination of Classical architecture lies therefore in beauty of expression, that of Gothic in strength of expression: the one speaks the language of organic being, the other the language of abstract values.

Posterity has seen in Gothic only logical values, and has had no perception for the super-logical, probably because it degrades this super-logical to the level of modern romanticism, thereby completely overlooking the logical values. If we put this romanticism aside, we discover that Gothic architecture was only appreciated as a structural achievement. It was particularly discredited by its decadent posterity, those champions of the neo-German " architect's Gothic," who plied their trade in the nineteenth century. Such an understanding of Gothic was literal only, not spiritual. As there was no longer any spiritual relation to the transcendental will to form, Gothic was only cherished for its structural and decorative values; and as restoration or as new construction that bare, lifeless, sober Gothic was created, which seems to have been conceived by a calculating machine instead of by the spirit.

The modern art of steel construction has first given to us again a certain inward understanding of Gothic. Here again people have been confronted with an architectural form in which the artistic expression is taken over by the medium of construction. But, in spite of all external affinities, a powerful internal difference can be observed, for in modern architecture it is the material itself which directly invites this, exclusively structural significance, while in Gothic the structural ideas were attained, not by means of the material, but in spite of the material, in spite of the stone. In other words: underlying the artistic appearance of the modern building constructed of steel there is no will to form which, for particular reasons, emphasizes structure, but only a new material. The utmost that might be said for it is that it is an atavistic echo of the old Gothic will to form which urges the modern Northern man to an artistic emphasis of this material and which even allows us to hope for a new style in architecture dependent on its relevant use.

In Gothic the need for expression was he prime factor and the material, stone, not only did not lend itself to this need, but was actually in opposition. It established itself in spite of being bound to the stone, and it thereby introduced a decisive new note into the development of an architecture which had been mainly an architecture of stone and as such had been either an organic articulation like the Greek, or a structureless mass like the Oriental, or a mixture of the two, like the Roman. That Gothic, after all these building methods which were direct embodiments of the tradition of stone construction, should create something absolutely new—namely the structural scaffold building, the *mechanically* articulated building, and, as such, the complete opposite of the *organically* articulated building—this is the achievement in which its highest and most individual striving for expression was realized.

XIV

THE VICISSITUDES
OF THE GOTHIC WILL TO FORM

Having learned how to recognize the general character of Northern Gothic will to form in its purest manifestations—early ornament and mature Gothic architecture—we will now investigate the vicissitudes of this will to form. We shall here be touching upon the great chapter in the development of mediaeval art, a chapter which, owing to the one-sidedness of the Renaissance point of view inherited by the modern historian, has never obtained its due.

These vicissitudes of Gothic will to form are chiefly determined, on the one hand, by its natural growth and increasing vigour, on the other by its adjustments to alien manifestations of style, amongst which, in addition to Oriental influences, Roman art with the classical tendency of its will to form comes most prominently under consideration. The interesting drama of the adjustment between North and South, Gothic and Classical, the rich content of which determines the whole import of the development of mediaeval art, begins with the first influence of Roman culture on the North, in the early centuries after Christ. Roman provincial art, the art of the migratory period, Merovingian art, Carolingian art, Romanesque art, and Gothic art (in the restricted academic meaning of the phrase)—these are the various acts of this drama. The last act shows us the collapse of Gothic and the submergence of the feeling for form of the Northern nations in the European structure of the Renaissance. The substance of these various acts can here be outlined only in brief.

The political and cultural supremacy of the Roman conquerors naturally postulated their artistic supremacy also. At first, the indigenous feeling for art yielded completely to this supremacy as manifested in Roman provincial art. It found no opportunity for activity in any sphere. It was only quite gradually that it dared to reappear and, as it were, sought to obtain its rights in unobtrusive places. In time, however, a Germanic-

Roman ornament came into existence, in which the Northern and the Roman elements were fairly evenly balanced. The old Northern linear motives begin to appear on all sides mingled with these motives of a foreign art, seeking to impress their soul upon the alien bodies. Indeed, the Northern will to form gradually felt itself so strong that it dared to assert its independence in the face of this invasion of Roman art. This independence is demonstrated, for instance, by its refusal of the characteristic element of Roman decorative art, the special vehicle of the Roman classical feeling for form, namely, the ornamental plant-motive. With but very few exceptions, this specifically organic creation was not admitted into the early composite Germanic-Roman art. The migratory period naturally further strengthened the mixed character of Northern artistic activity. The most varied influences intersect each other, everything is in fermentation, the most incongruous elements stand side by side, but in the midst of all this medley, the expansive urge of the Northern feeling for form can never be overlooked. The characteristic hardness of this semi-barbaric, semi-Roman product proves that the struggle is no longer a secret guerilla warfare, but an open contest in which each party asserts its position. Hence the powerful magnificence of this style. The Merovingian period with its parallel Anglo-Saxon, Irish, Scandinavian, and North Italian manifestations shows that the Northern feeling for form had definitely won the day. It brought with it the true blossoming of that linear fantasy, permeated with elements of reality, which, for the reason that it offers the best foundation for the investigation of the entire phenomenon of style, we have exhaustively discussed in a former chapter. In the Merovingian period, however, plant-motives had already penetrated into Northern ornament: under the influence of the Carolingian Renaissance the old indigenous animal ornament begins to give place to this new plant ornament. But here it is a question of a movement which possessed no native soil of its own: the Carolingian Renaissance was an experiment emanating from the Court, which found no hold in the popular consciousness. This premature experiment brought the Northern feeling for art into a transient condition of complete disorientation, which only yielded to a slowly growing feeling of security at the end of the period. And this points the way to an estimation of this interesting intermezzo. We can adopt the verdict of Woermann: " Apart from a few creations in the sphere of architecture, a few examples of goldsmiths' work and a few decorated pages, devoid of figures, in book illumination, Carolingian-Othonian art produced nothing which posterity could take up again. It was itself pre-eminently the art of a posterity, whose language of form and colour, in spite of its profound and extensive content, in spite of its often splendid general outward effect, was merely a barbaric stammering in the accents of a past irrecoverably lost and moreover racially alien to the Germanic North. The immature, natural accents seeking half unconsciously to make themselves heard here and there die away, unheard for a long time. It is only quite towards the end of this period that they are heard more clearly and more frequently."

To the succeeding phase in the process of development, the Romanesque style, we shall have to devote a more searching attention, for it already represents that Mediaevalism, now arrived at its full strength and independent consciousness of culture, under which North-West Europe had energetically taken into its hands the reins of development. As we shall pay particular attention to architectural development, we shall here merely point out that the Romanesque style is a very radical and happy modification, with a Northern feeling, of the forms and motives inherited from the ancient East. In spite of the dependence of its basic structure on antique tradition, it exhibits a pronounced Northern character. The Basilica form, imposed from an alien art upon the North by the cultural dominance of Rome and her ecclesiastical sovereignty, is already seen to be completely permeated with the Gothic will to form, which in its task of imbuing this alien form with its own soul and spirit, continually grew in strength, until finally, in the frenzy of energy of the great Gothic centuries, it resolutely abandoned altogether the alien form and created for itself its own magnificent world of expression, which opposed to antique tradition something entirely new and independent. This is actual Gothic, Gothic in the narrower academic sense of the term, the final emancipation from everything classical.

And with this, its highest and purest development, the Northern feeling for form conquered the whole of Europe. In the adjustment arrived at between North and South, the real purport of all mediaeval development, the North at this period has triumphed, both culturally and artistically. But it seems as if this supreme exertion had exhausted it. Northern will to form, having reached its zenith, had played itself out: it had reached the limit of its formative possibilities. Its mission was accomplished, and the Romance peoples of the South who, meanwhile, had recovered politically as well as culturally from the irruption of the North, and had collected their scattered energies for a new civilization and a new art, had an easy task with the North which had spent its forces. Now that the Northern formative energy had slackened, that reverberation followed which the experiment of the Carolingian Renaissance had failed to set up. Cultural supremacy decided the victory. For mediaeval culture, which so far had known no differentiation of the individual—for the individual only dares to separate himself from the mass when dualistic fears have been overcome and a state of equilibrium and security in the relationship between the world and man has been attained—was now faced with a new culture, which had released all the resources of the individual and had created values of intellectual progress that, unrestricted by any dogmatic constraint, must have presented a tempting ideal to Northern man bound down as he had been during the Middle Ages. In his craving for liberation which, exhausted by prodigious displays of energy, had lost its great driving power, he believed that he would now find satisfaction in such direct objectivity. Northern transcendentalism ebbed away into mere Transalpinism, to a cultural Ultramontanism. The same dualistic distraction, which had lulled itself to quiescence in the great transcendental art of the Middle Ages, now urged Northern man towards the alien Renaissance ideal. He had sought to submerge his inward wretchedness, his spiritual dissatisfaction, in the exalted pathos of Gothic, in its unnatural convulsive tension, in its powerful frenzy of sensation, but the strength to meet such tension had only been found in the compact mass. Now that economic developments, world intercourse, civic life, and other cultural factors had exercised their attraction upon the great collective masses, even in the North, a more intimate, human satisfaction had to be sought. Gothic, by its inmost nature, had been irrational, super-rational, transcendental: now the intensified rationalism of classical harmony and classical conformity to law presented itself as an alluring ideal to Northern man turned individual; he now hoped that, as he no longer had strength for the ideal exuberance of transcendental will power, he would be able to get free from himself and deliver himself from his wretchedness in this ideal ratio by means of this so distant, almost unattainable classical harmony. An immediate satisfaction, a direct naive happiness is denied him, his happiness lies always—and this is the true Northern transcendentalism which has remained the same through the centuries—in otherworldliness, a getting beyond himself, whether it consist in exaltation of ecstasy or in clinging to an alien ideal. All the time he finds himself only by losing himself, by going out beyond himself, and from this dilemma spring both his greatness and his tragedy.

The qualitative difference between Gothic transcendentalism and the later Northern Ultramontanism (Romanism) can also be explained by saying that with the coming of the Renaissance religious ideals were replaced by purely intellectual ideals. In any case, the entire culture of the German Renaissance bears the odium of being an intellectual product, lacking direct natural premises. This applies also to post-Gothic art. That, too, is more an offspring of culture than the direct product of real, original, artistic sensation and purpose. The morbid Northern craving for culture, that disguised and weakened form of transcendentalism, subjugates the Northern instinct for form, and the result is the hybrid product of the German Renaissance, or, in the sphere of culture, of German humanism. Art is partly veiled in literary forms and partly silted up with external decoration. Instead of a strong unconscious will, it is now a conscious, artistic taste which is at work. These characteristics of the German Renaissance naturally apply only to the generality of cases, to the great public art, which was more especially inaugurated by Cranach. In the case of great individual artists such as Dürer, Grünewald, or Holbein, things are otherwise. When their work is minutely examined, it is seen that it is all closely allied to Gothic. Grünewald's Gothic has an air of picturesque pathos, Holbein's graphic capacity for characterization is—as we have already remarked in another connection—the final great concentration of Northern linear art. And Dürer? Albrecht Dürer became an absolute martyr to this clash of two worlds of artistic expression which were fundamentally incompatible. This it is which gives the great note of tragedy to the whole course of his development. That he was unable to relinquish himself, his Northern humanity, whilst nevertheless with his discordant temperament he struggled with all his powers to attain this new world, whose starting-point and goal were harmony and beauty, this was the tragedy which made him so great and made him the true representative of the North. For this is a specifically Northern tragedy, which repeats itself ever in new shapes and disguises, and whose last martyr, to take an example from the present with which we are most familiar, we Northern men honour in Hans von Marées, with his great fragmentary, enigmatic art.

The victorious advance of the classical feeling for form in the wake of the great Italian Renaissance movement left the Gothic will to form no time to ebb quietly away into itself. The suppressed Gothic energies of form, however, rooted in so mighty a past, were still far too active beneath the surface to disappear noiselessly from the scene. Humanism, contemplative and alien to reality, the privilege of generously endowed lives, could not permanently keep down the fermenting, popular conscious-ness of development then prevailing. It was corrected by that great, popular movement which led to the Reformation. Religious ideals once more replaced intellectual ideals, humanism was ousted by the Reformation. The reaction against the humanistic intellectual ideal with its classical heathen colouring ran through the whole of Europe, manifesting itself artistically in the phenomenon of the Baroque style. The transcendental character of this style is demonstrated externally by the very fact that churches, more especially Jesuit churches, were the propagators and vehicles of it. Its transcendental pathos separates it distinctly from the harmonious restfulness and equilibrium of the classical style. The transcendental Gothic style, followed by the intermezzo of the Renais-sance, is succeeded by another transcendental style, the Baroque. And in Northern Baroque, it is believed, a distinct connection between this style and Gothic may be traced—especially if late Gothic, which has been called significantly the Baroque of Gothic, is called to mind. The Northern Renaissance forms did not long retain their moderation. They quickly developed into restless, crowded scroll-work, and it seems as if the old, suppressed, Gothic energies of form were at work, disturbing and expanding this alien organic world of art. The Gothic, pathetic force of will seems to have been transfused into this organic world of expression. Vitalized and stirred by this ever-growing influx of Northern will-impulse, the forms of German Renaissance art by degrees lose altogether that harmonious impress which in them was rather lack of character than, as in the Italian Renaissance, positive expression of will; they lose that harmonious smoothness and once again the flood of Northern will to art, contemptuous of all harmonious measure, surges through the world. Again everything is movement, everything is thronging activity and pathos. But this pathos can only be expressed through the utmost enhancement and tension of the organic values; the way back to the higher and more rapturous pathos of abstract, transcendental values is blocked by the Renaissance. Thus, in Baroque, we see the last welling up of Northern will to form, a final urge for self-expression even in an inappropriate language essentially alien to it. And then the tones of the old Northern art of line and movement slowly die away in the playful scroll-work of the Rococo.

I comply with the necessity of recapitulating once more in conclusion the course of development outlined in this chapter by quoting a passage from an academy lecture delivered by Alexander Conze, the Berlin archaeologist: " In the meaningless play of form of their geometrical style, untold generations of the old European nations found satisfaction for their aesthetic needs in the domain of plastic art, until gradually, under Southern influences, they were drawn into the circle of a richer world of form derived from one of the countries in the Eastern corner of the Mediterranean. But their own peculiar artistic sensibility did not thereby finally become extinct with the same rapidity as that of savages who nowadays come into much more violent contact with more highly developed civilization. In Greece, the Doric style, in which as Taine says ' trois ou quatre formes élémentaires de la géometrie font tous les frais,' may have grown up under the after effects of the mood of the old geometric style. But in the North of Europe the vitality of primeval habit shows itself unmistakably when confronted with the intrusion of Graeco-Roman art. After its first submission, the old native fashion pushes its way through, remodelling the alien forms, to issue in the Gothic style as the radiant outcome of the struggle between the two worlds of art; and even in the Rococo, after the repeated triumphs of the Renaissance, a last dying echo of it may be imagined. In Moslem art, an analogous breaking out of early undercurrents through the Graeco-

Roman surface went on side by side with the emergence of the Gothic style. Such far-reaching considerations, however, could only be developed in full with reference to the world-historical elements in the general history of art " (*Sitzungsbericht der Berliner Akademie der Wissenschaften*, 11, II, 1897).

35.   Sculptured tympanum.   Vézelay (plaster cast)

36. St. Timothy. Glass-painting, Cluny Museum, Paris
(*photo: Ellen Vieyra*)

37. Virtue combating Vice
Glass-painting, Mühlhausen.
(*photo: Courtesy Dr. Hans Wentzel*)

38. Christ on the Cross
Swabian glass-painting.
(*photo: Courtesy Dr. Hans Wertzel*)

39. Mourning figure from
the Lamentation over the
Dead Christ.
Cathedral Museum, Limburg.
(*from: Back. Mittelrheinische
Kunst, Verlag J. Baer & Co.*)

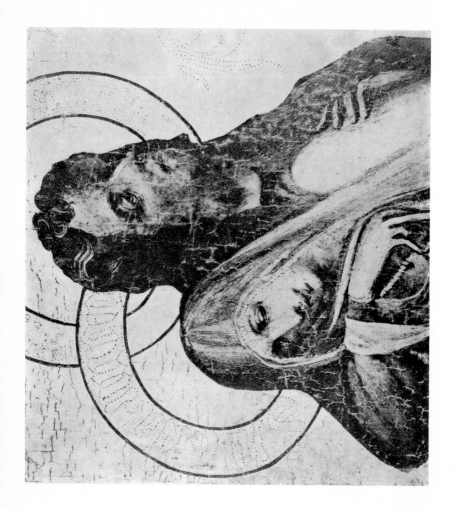

40. The Virgin and St. John. Detail of a Crucifixion. Church of St. Stephen, Mainz. (from: Back, Mittelrheinische Kunst, Verlag J. Baer & Co.)

41. Entombment.
Detail from altar-piece.
Church of St. James,
Göttingen, about 1400.
(courtesy: Deutsches
Verein für Kunstwissen-
schaft, Berlin)

42.   Annunciation
Cologne School. Wallraf-Richartz-Museum, Cologne

XV

THE ROMANESQUE STYLE

The entire history of the vicissitudes of Gothic will to form may be reduced to two consecutive, principal stages, to which all else is subordinated. The first of these stages was that of the decorative, the second that of the architectural activity, of the will to form. Just as ornament represented the true embodiment of the Gothic artistic faculty in the development of early Northern Gothic, so in its later development architecture was its true representative. If in reality but one single will to form existed as a basis for all artistic effort from the first Christian centuries until the late Middle Ages, the aim of this development must have been to vary the ponderous, elementary laws of architecture in such a way, so to differentiate them and make them elastic, as to enable them to express the feeling for form contained in free ornament. And it is indeed the most brilliant chapter in the development of mediaeval art, showing us how this feeling for form, corresponding to the spiritual structure of Northern man, which had originally manifested itself only in ornament unfettered by purpose and the requirements of material, gradually made itself master of the heavy, intractable substance and, despite its material resistance, compelled it to become the selfless, tractable instrument of its expression.

Our information as to the pagan temple of the North is scanty, and the flood of controversy which still rages concerning the Northern wood architecture of the pre-Christian era and its relation to the Northern religious buildings of Christian times, does not as yet permit any definite decision to be made concerning these questions. There is, however, one point which admits of no argument: early Northern architecture was already dominated by the will to the perpendicular, by the tendency to create vertical and not horizontal buildings. Of the two basic elements of tectonics, active support and passive weight, the adjustment of which in Greek architecture had culminated in a happy state of organic equilibrium, Northern architecture from the outset gave the preference to the first;

the expression of activity was to predominate; the building must appear as freely rising and not as pressed down by weight.

The true mediaeval architectural development only begins with the acceptance of Christianity, which demanded an adjustment to the classical idea of construction embodied in Early Christian architecture. This severance it was which primarily compelled the North to evolve a characteristic stone edifice, and first brought its sluggish and arbitrary sense of architectural form face to face with the decisive test. And it stood the test. To avoid bringing into question by a diffuse, detailed exposition the terse, pregnant character of the line of development laid down, we will pass over the initial stages of this adjustment. The Carolingian buildings also need but a passing reference, as being an isolated experiment somewhat remote from the true line of development. Its true significance first finds expression in the so-called Romanesque style. The character of this style as regards psychological form will now be analysed in order that one may then learn to comprehend the crowning stage of this development in the mature Gothic style.

By Romanesque style we mean the modification in style which the imported Early Christian scheme of construction underwent at the hands of the independent will to art of the North. By establishing the details of th's modification, we can watch, as it were, the working of the Gothic will to form. For all the changes it imposed upon the alien artistic form represented by the basilica are indications of the later, true Gothic development in which it completely emancipated itself from this alien form.

The Romanesque style of architecture represents the stage in the adjustment of Northern and antique artistic feeling roughly corresponding in the evolution of ornament to the style of the Migration of the Peoples. It is instinct with the same seriousness, grand and full of character, the same heavy magnificence of material, which result from two spheres of art existing in frank, uncompromising juxtaposition, without any trace of interpenetration. The strength of each seems to be attuned to that of the other, so that in spite of this unyielding co-existence, a certain uniformity of impression is realized. Romanesque architecture has style, because the adjustment is honest and straightforward and one in which each element firmly holds its ground. In so far as it was possible for the Northern will to art to assert itself without abandoning the inherited scheme of the basilica, dependent upon antique tradition, it succeeded in so doing.

We have seen that the Gothic will to form was the striving towards unfettered activity, towards expressive movement of an immaterial nature. If we now compare a Romanesque cathedral with an Early Christian basilica, the outward structure shows us at once what this Northern will to expression has evolved from the basilica plan. The Early Christian basilica has a homogeneous accent. The homogeneous, longitudinal movement towards the choir is quite clearly indicated externally as well. In the Romanesque style, this simple elementary scheme of the basilica undergoes a thoroughgoing articulation which suppresses its uniformity and substitutes a rich diversity for simplicity devoid of charm: for the single accent, a multitude of accents possessing a certain rhythmic restraint. It is as if an objective, logically constructed Latin sentence were compared with a verse from the Song of Hildebrand with its restless, rugged, uncommonly expressive rhythm, its almost too exuberant wealth of accent. This ponderous, compressed structure of phrase, almost bursting under the pressure of the movement crowded into it, enables us to comprehend the ponderousness and compression of the Romanesque style of architecture. Movement is activity. The impulse for articulation in Romanesque architecture is no other than the Gothic need for activity, which desires to remould and to differentiate, in accordance with its own spirit, the serene, externally quite objective and meagrely expressive form of the Early Christian basilica. The essentials of Romanesque architecture are generally discussed from the standpoint of pictorial,[1] that is, two-dimensional, appearance, which means confusing cause and effect. For this pictorial appearance is merely the secondary effect of those primary manifestations of activity which express themselves in articulation. For, as this need for activity articulates the expressionless homogeneity of appearance, extracting individual forces from the lifeless objective mass, it transforms repose into movement and replaces simplicity by multiplicity. And pictorial effect is the natural

[1] This seems to be the only possible rendering of " malerisch "; this word, sometimes synonymous with the English word " picturesque," is here used to distinguish two-dimensional from plastic art. [ED.]

result of this restless movement and variety. Northern architecture retains this pictorial character only as long as Northern energies of form were obliged to develop on the basis of the early mass construction. Here the pictorial effect owes its existence merely to the opposition of the lifeless mass to the division into members brought about by the energy to form of the North. As soon as this basis disappears and the members, with their expression of activity, no longer clash against a background of lifeless mass (that is to say, in the true Gothic), the relief character of the Romanesque style vanishes; in other words, its pictorial effect ceases to exist. Pure Gothic is undeniably full of activity but without any real pictorial effect; which clearly proves that the pictorial effect of Romanesque style is not an end in itself, but merely the outcome of a need for activity still adjusting itself to the Roman architectural style of mass and wall. The exceedingly pictorial effect of the style of the period of the Wanderings of the Peoples is based on the same presuppositions.

These remarks apply to the profuse articulation of the ground plan as well as to the articulation of the exterior. The external aspect is dominated by a combined system of blind arcading and pilaster strips which breaks up into life and movement the walls of lifeless masonry. This vitality is still a thing apart from the actual structure of the building; it is only outwardly superimposed, a merely decorative accessory. This accumulated organic expression of vitality manifested by the shafted arcades which give life to the walls, produces the effect of being a kind of makeshift for the strong Northern craving for expression which had not yet discovered its own peculiar means of expression, that is to say, a super-organic constructive language. For, as regards construction, the Romanesque style was still bound up with the antique scheme. Consequently the Northern will to form could only find expression on lines parallel to this basic architectural structure, instead of combining with it, as the Gothic did. The expenditure of an external indirect expansion of strength, which, in accordance with the fundamental idea of the structure, still made use of organic means of expression, had to fill the place of the direct inner expansion of strength which was lacking. Connected with this is the trend of the Romanesque style towards Baroque degeneracy. For we may consider as Baroque all manifestations of style exhibiting an organic life under the strain of an excessive pressure. And this

excessive pressure invariably occurs when the right valves are blocked
up, thus preventing the proper liberation—when the organic possibilities
of expression have to overpower a vital force which actually exceeds
their strength and which can only be subjugated by super-organic
forces. And the Romanesque style is as far removed from abstract
super-organic, that is, true Gothic, possibilities of expression as is the
Baroque style, with this exception, that in the one case the way was still
barred in consequence of dependence upon the antique tradition, and
in the other, as a result of the revival and absolute predominance of this
identical antique tradition, the way was again blotted out. Like the
Baroque, the Romanesque style was an attempt at a Gothic style carried
out with inefficient, that is, only with purely organic, means. And it is
increasingly borne in upon our consciousness that the Renaissance was
merely a kind of foreign body introduced into this amazing and otherwise uninterrupted development, which leads from the earliest Northern
beginnings to the Baroque and even further, to the Rococo.

The extended nave of the basilica gives the whole edifice externally
a recumbent appearance. In view of the preference of the Northern will to
art for the creation of erect, upward-soaring buildings which gave an
impression of unchecked activity, it was evident that the broad, recumbent
form of the Basilica would meet with opposition. It was necessary at all
costs to wrest from it a development into height. This effort resulted
in the Romanesque system of multiple towers, which substitutes a vertical
accentuation already of considerable strength for the horizontal accentuation of the basilica. Even here it is still an attempt made with unservice-
able means. The towers are dumped on in more or less arbitrary fashion:
their upward energy does not grow directly out of the internal structure
of the edifice; consequently, being deprived of this constructional
elasticity, they cannot dispel the impression of material heaviness. Here
again the redeeming word remains unspoken; and so what was denied
to direct realization was attempted by a multiplicity, an accumulation of
effects. The change could only come from within. The new birth
could only take shape in the inmost womb of the edifice. And directly
that was accomplished, directly the decisive word had been given, the
external form of the edifice came about quite automatically. The building
had first to find its own soul in order to emancipate itself from the body

and to liberate the Gothic impulse towards height, this urge towards an endless, immaterial agitation.

This emancipation from the body, that is to say, the emancipation from the entire sensuous building conception of the antique tradition, begins in the Romanesque style with the first attempts at vaulting. With the first attempts at vaulting, the Northern builder penetrated to the very core of the antique architectural form, which, so far, he had left untouched.

We will deal with this decisive advance in a special chapter.

XVI

THE BEGINNINGS OF EMANCIPATION FROM THE IDEA OF CLASSICAL ARCHITECTURE

Stimulated by the Orient, antique architecture in Hellenistic, and still more in Roman times, had concerned itself in a thoroughgoing manner with the problem of vaulting; and Roman provincial art had left behind on Northern soil imposing examples of its solutions. But the mediaeval art of vaulting now beginning had nothing in common artistically with this antique Classical vaulting tradition: the relations between the two were merely technical. It would be easier to find artistic connections with the Oriental tradition of vaulting which, like the later Northern, had aimed at pictorial space-formation. But that would take us too far. To understand the fundamental difference between the classical and the Gothic-Northern idea of vaulting, we must be quite clear as to what artistic aims were served by Classical vaulting. The genesis of Classical vaulting is intimately connected with the development of the formation of interiors, initiated in the Hellenistic and reaching its climax in the Roman period. We have seen that in Greek times space, as such, played no artistic part: we recognized Greek architecture as being purely tectonic without any intentional creation of space. In the Hellenistic period, Greek sensibility suffers the loss of its plastic quality, which was entirely directed towards the substantial and concrete: by contact with the Orient it was permeated with non-sensuous spiritual elements and in due course the art of space-creation was evolved from tectonics. We have already discussed these connections elsewhere. But even with this intentional creation of spaces, the actual antique remains classical, that is to say, it approaches space with organic creation as its aim and endeavours to treat it as something organically living, even as something corporeal. In other words: clarity of space, as the ideal of Roman architecture, takes the place of clarity of form as the ideal of Greek tectonics; organic space-creation replaces organic form-creation; instead of form-sculpture comes space-sculpture, if this bold expression (which is, however, entirely appropriate to the conditions) may be permitted. The limits of the space should be such as to convey that the space had, as it were of itself, defined them, to mark its individuality as compared with infinite space. The impression must be given of natural limitations of space, within which the space itself may lead an independent, organically circumscribed life. Thus the non-sensuous, that is, space, again becomes sensualized, the immaterial is materialized, the intangible is made objective. These artistic aims were served by the Classical art of space, whose most brilliant achievement was the Pantheon. Vaulting here is merely a means for the realization of a sensuous space-sculpture, whose ideal it is to create, with spatial relationships, the impression of a life harmonious, peaceful, and adjusted to itself. In this harmonious structure of space, the struggle between the supporting and burdening energies has now entirely ceased. What Greek tectonics could attain only indirectly, that is to say, by means of the entire system of symbolic intervening members, namely, the softening of the constructively unavoidable clash of weight and energy, the sensuous space-culture of the Roman attains directly by the art of vaulting: the vaulting gathers all the supporting energies into itself in soft organic curves, and without any violence leads them to a calm, obvious conclusion and equipoise. It would be difficult to decide whether such an architectonic structure as the Pantheon rises from the ground or whether it rests upon it; indeed, owing to the absolutely organic formation of space these impressions of support and burden neutralize one another: the supporting and burdening energies are in a perfect state of equilibrium.

Thus in Roman art we see that vaulting—putting aside its purely practical importance in useful buildings—is the result of a certain sensuous space-sculpture and therefore bears a distinctly classical character.

Our entire survey of the non-sensuous Gothic will to art already shows us the way to recognition of quite different artistic requirements, which the mediaeval art of vaulting had to meet. This is not the result of any kind of organic, sensuous plastic tendency; it rather serves a super-sensuous striving for expression which knows nothing of the concept of harmony. It has nothing to do with an adjustment between supporting and burdening energies, active and passive energies, vertical and horizontal energies, but the activity, the verticality alone was to carry out the artistic expression. The overcoming of weight by a freely soaring, self-controlled activity, the subjugation of matter by an immaterial expression of movement—that is the goal which presents itself to the mediaeval art of vaulting, the goal it reached in mature Gothic. In mature Gothic one can hardly speak of a burdening roof. The intuition of and feeling for the upper termination of the space is only created by the union of the unburdened vertical energies crowding in from every side and allowing the movement to die away as it were in the infinite. Not until we keep this aim before our eyes can we estimate the importance of the first attempts at vaulting in Northern architecture in their full, pregnant significance. It is only then that, behind the technical progress, we first observe the will to form struggling for the expression which makes it an artistic advance as well.

In our consideration of the subject we shall entirely put aside the question of borrowed architectural forms. The question of borrowing only becomes acute when alien forms oppose the native will to form; and then it is no longer a question of borrowing but of an independent reproduction. For knowledge of what is alien serves at most as a signal to bring to utterance the as yet undecided and hesitating will to form. Thus it only provokes and hastens that which is already outlined and ripe for expression in the inward line of development. These external elements cannot therefore alter the inner course of development; consequently observation which is entirely devoted to this inward, as it were subterranean development, may completely disregard these irrelevant external elements.

The development began with the most obvious, and technically simplest, embodiment of the principle of vaulting, the barrel vault. With it came the first attack on the roof and its weight. But the organically compact form of this undifferentiated, expressionless, constructively unaccented kind of vaulting, offered no possibility of application and activity to the abstract craving for expression of the Northern will to art. To the non-sensuous Northern feeling for art, this evenly curved form, in which there was no distinction between active and passive energies and which was therefore constructively unaccented, was simply an inanimate mass. An effort had to be made to extract definite accents frcm the unbroken coherence of the vaulting, to give to the vaulted mass a structural expression of activity, answering to the Gothic need for expression. Cross-vaulting more nearly met these artistic requirements; consequently, in the Romanesque style, it reached a pre-eminence which it had possessed at no other time. For the entire treatment of cross-vaulting in Roman times, especially from the decorative point of view, proves that it was not affected for the structural play of its liveliness of expression, but for its great technical advantages. Worthy of note is the fact that the South of France, with its uninterrupted antique tradition, never definitely accepted cross-vaulting, although the imposing Roman vaulted buildings in that region provided the most instructive examples for the technical perfecting of vault constructions. Southern France never came to adopt cross-vaulting: it remained faithful to the barrel vault, giving it a monumental form which was technically of the utmost refinement. It did not take this step because cross-vaulting was in opposition to the French feeling for form, coloured as it still was by antique tradition. But the nearer we ccme to Central and Northern France, the more the Germanic leaven in the mixture of races asserts itself, the more strongly do we see the cross-vault predominating, reaching its apogee in Norman architecture. How forcibly, on the other hand, cross-vaulting ran contrary to the classical will to form, is best demonstrated by the dislike evinced by the Renaissance for this form of vaulting, a dislike which has been specially emphasized by Burckhardt. Nevertheless, cross-vaulting was still constantly used, it is true, but surreptitiously, or else the convincing mimicry of expression in its structure was taken from it as in Roman times by coffering or by other decorative details.

But cross-vaulting met the Northern will to form more than half-way. For in contrast with the mass of the barrel-vault, to Northern sensibility dead and uniform, a clear, comprehensive articulation was here already in being. Here the vaulting process at once appears as action. A uniform accent of height attains pronounced expression at the point of intersection of the four sectroids, and this accentuation of the crown of the vault imparts to the whole, in spite of its actual compression, the illusion of soaring towards the centre. The pronouncedly active character of the cross-vault distinguishes it from the barrel-vault which was completely undifferentiated as regards activity and passivity. This impression of

136

activity is determined especially by the groins in which the sectroids of the vault come together: they give to the vaulting a linear play quite in keeping with the Northern will to art. It is comprehensible that the further development embodied in Gothic should begin with this groined construction. The first step was to emphasize this linear play by supplementing the groined arches with ribs which had at first no inward connection with the vaulting, but besides being intended as supports, served to intensify the linear expression. The Romans had already used this ribbing as reinforcement, but it is significant that in their case " the reinforcement was of more importance during the process of erection than for the completed building " (Dehio and Bezold). In other words: with the Romans, the ribbing reinforcement played a merely practical and not an artistic part; it was only a means to an end. But in Romanesque art it is also an end in itself and the vehicle of artistic expression. On the other hand, German architecture shows many examples—they are of especially frequent occurrence in Westphalia—in which the ribs are applied to the finished vaulting, thus plainly showing themselves to be mere decorative members, that is to say, purely mimic vehicles of expression.

The second great decisive step in the development of groining is that whereby the inner constitution of the vault was allowed to be hidden by this linear play. It is the great Gothic revolution in the vaulting system, whereby the ribs of the vaulting were converted into actual supports of the vault construction, and the intervals of vault surface were inserted merely as a filling for the framework. The ribs become the innermost scaffold of the entire structure: the artistic meaning of the ribs becomes one with their structural meaning. And we shall see how incessantly this procedure, so decisive for the entire Gothic problem, is repeated; how the Gothic craving for expression can at first only manifest itself externally, can find utterance only decoratively as it were beyond the structure, until at last it finds the language in which alone it can express itself convincingly, namely, the abstract, non-sensuous language of construction. Then all obstacles to utterance fall away and the pure, unalloyed fulfilment of the faculty for expression is guaranteed.

More or less consciously, this idea of allowing construction to be an aim in itself, of making it the vehicle of artistic expression, was present in the mind of the Northern architect when he adopted the pier as a supporting member and made it gradually supplant the column. This supplanting process was not a rapid one: the power of suggestion in the antique tradition was too strong to permit of an immediate disappearance of the column, that true representative of antique architecture. It was at first only timidly that the pier dared to assert itself beside it, until finally it was evident that to the pier the future of the development belonged. And it was more especially in regions far removed from the scene of Roman influence, and consequently less subject to its antique after-suggestion, that the basilica with piers soon played a predominant part.

It is quite easy to see why the Northern artistic feeling rebelled against the column and preferred the pier. The structural function of support is organically demonstrated in the column, but for that organic demonstration the Northern feeling lacked the cultured sensuousness of the antique. On the other hand, the pier is a perfectly objective form exercising the function of support without any value of expression. But it is just that objective-constructive character of the pier which offered to the Northern craving for abstract expression a possibility for self-assertion totally different from that afforded by the column, which was bound up with the world of organic expression.

The fact that the rectangular pier had already appeared in early Romanesque times proves that it was accepted at first only because its configuration satisfied the Northern craving for expression. That its appearance coincides with the first attempts at vaulting, as has been generally said, is not correct. Nevertheless, because of the tendencies towards vaulting, the outward preference for it has a certain inward technical justification; that is to say, in view of its purpose, the mere artistic significance of vaulting obtains a constructive sanction as well. For, as in the cross-vault the pressure of the vaulting is not equal, but is concentrated on the four outer angles, a more powerful support was needed for this vault-pressure concentrated at the lower angles than the weak column could offer. The pier therefore offered itself as the appropriate substitute for the column.

Owing, however, to this structural connection between vaulting and pier, the pier imperceptibly begins to lose its objective character. The latent expression it contains is, as it were, awakened by the intimate connection in which it stands with the girths and ribs of the vaulting. It has ceased to be an objective supporting member as it was in the flat-roofed basilica. After it has found contact with the vaulted roof by means of attached columns, which gather up the vaulting ribs, its vital energy seems to awaken, it no longer seems to support but to soar upward. It takes part as an active member in the general vertical movement in process of development, and the constructive connection between pier and vaulting system begins to speak out in a clear, convincing play.

It is this straightforward return to the constructive basic elements of building, abandoning all the antique arts of translation into the organic, which gives its impress to the inner structure of the Romanesque cathedral. It is perceptible in both great things and small. In the sphere of individual detail one may call to mind the formation of the Romanesque capital. A comparison between a Romanesque cushion capital with its clear tectonic form, and an antique capital, best shows perhaps the tendency of the Romanesque architect to return to clear, constructive objectivity. It is a more negative process which manifests itself in all this, a process necessary to clear the way for the future development. The structure had first to be freed in its objectivity from all the sensuous additions amalgamated with it by the classical will to art, the constructive energies had as it were to be rallied, before it became possible with these energies alone to attain to the great artistic expression of the Middle Ages.

In Romanesque architecture, therefore, the structure has, it is true, already been disengaged, but it has not yet been intensified; the great Gothic pathos has not yet appeared: the Romanesque style is a Gothic without enthusiasm, a Gothic still subservient to material weight, a Gothic without the final, transcendental liberation. Recourse was had to logic but without as yet pursuing with its aid any super-logical aim. This seriousness, which is in some degree heaviness, this objectivity, which to a certain extent is sobriety, this compressed and restrained apparent weight which has a solemn but not a transporting effect, fore-ordained the Romanesque style to be the true Protestant-German style; and it is not therefore by chance that modern Protestant church architecture by preference resumes the thread of the Romanesque style. The half-way, hybrid character which is the fault of Protestantism, this vacillation between rationalistic-scholastic and metaphysical elements, between strict adherence to the word and individual freedom: all this is reflected also in the Romanesque style. It is also full of inner contradictions. Thus, it is in part already Gothic scaffolding-style, in part still antique mass-style, yet, on the other hand, in spite of the firmly restrained character of the ground plan, it exhibits an arbitrariness which leads Dehio to lay down that symmetry, in its strictest form, was absolutely displeasing to Romanesque style and was therefore always broken by it, slightly or more decisively. In no other style are strict restraint and arbitrariness so closely connected as in the Romanesque style; in no religion do they lie so close together as in Protestantism.

The German character of the Romanesque style distinguishes it plainly from the international, universal Gothic. The Romanesque style is the style pertaining to the strongly Germanic countries where foreign strains are almost absent: it is most firmly rooted in Normandy, Burgundy, Lombardy, and finally in Germany proper. Its florescence is closely connected with the great days of German Imperial domination. Its period of splendour also came to an end with the downfall of this Imperial power.

XVII

COMPLETE EMANCIPATION IN PURE GOTHIC

We have seen how in the Romanesque style the Northern-Gothic form-energies had already become independent, how in fullness of character they asserted their place by the side of the antique tradition. We have, however, also seen how they continued in this juxtaposition, how they lacked the power of persisting to the end and completing their emancipation from that tradition. For this great and decisive act, an enthusiasm and an impulse of will were needed, which the peoples of predominantly Germanic character, with their ponderousness, were unable to compass. Their dull, chaotic striving remained fettered by tradition and material, they lacked the great decisive impetus to liberate themselves from this subjection; therefore the Romanesque style only presents a picture of suppressed, confined, restrained energy.

The shock which was to liberate this energy had to come from without. It was Romance Western Europe upon which this function devolved. The West provided the undecided Northern will to art with the great initiative which was to lead it to complete freedom. The Germanic North in its ponderousness had always been incapable of formulating independently what it dimly conceived and desired; it was always Western Europe, dominated by Romance elements, which shattered the law of Northern sluggishness, and which, in a great welling up of its energies, uttered the word which was waiting to be spoken by the Germanic North.

It was in the heart of France, where Germanic and Romance elements interpenetrated most closely, that the act of liberation was performed, that the signal was given which ushered in the true Gothic. Romance enthusiasm, which can be worked up to the highest pitch of tension without losing its clarity, finds a clear formula for the vague Northern will, in other words: it creates the Gothic system.

Nevertheless France cannot be called the actual home of Gothic;

Gothic itself did not arise in France, only the Gothic system. For the Romance elements of the country, which made France capable of this energy of initiative and this energy of clear formulation, had, on the other hand, kept alive the connection with the antique tradition and its organically coloured will to art. After the initial enthusiasm had died down, after the Romance elements had responded to the incentive to clear formulation which came from the Germanic North, with a great effort of energy, with a mighty accomplishment which was decisive for all Gothic, its mission was, one might say, fulfilled, and a state of self-consciousness set in, while this classical feeling for art, which had for the time being been entirely repressed by the great mediaëval task, announced itself once again. This land of happiest mingling of races was no abiding home for Gothic exclusiveness. The Romance delight in decorative completeness, in sensuous lucidity and organic harmony kept too strongly under repression the Germanic need for exaggeration, for excess. And this is why even the finest and most mature Gothic buildings in France are pervaded by an unmistakable atmosphere of organically clarified Renaissance feeling. Complete verticality is never attained, it is invariably counterbalanced by horizontal accentuations. Therefore it may be said that France created the most beautiful and most living Gothic buildings but not the purest. The land of pure Gothic culture is the Germanic North. And the assertion made at the beginning of our investigations is so far justified, that the true architectonic fulfilment of Northern will to form is to be found in German Gothic. It is true that English architecture is also tinged with Gothic; in a certain sense; it is true that England, which was too self-contained and isolated to be so much disturbed in its own artistic will by the Renaissance as was Germany, affects Gothic as its national style right down to the present day. But this English Gothic lacks the direct impulse of German Gothic, it lacks its strong pathos intensified by breaking against obstacles. English Gothic is more reserved, one might almost say more phlegmatic, and therefore easily incurs the danger of appearing frozen and sterile. And above all, it is more superficial, more trivial than German Gothic. What in the latter has the effect of an inward necessity, seems in English Gothic more or less arbitrary decoration.

In spite of the incontestable fact that Gothic was most firmly rooted

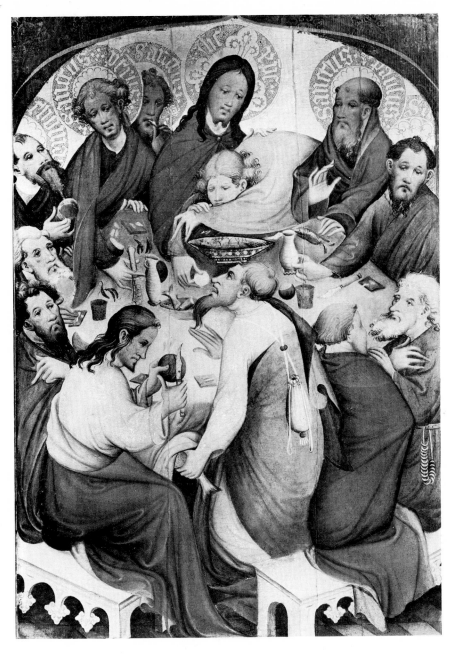

43. Konrad von Soest, The Last Supper
Centre panel of the High Altar at Wildungen
(*photo: Bildarchiv Foto Marburg*)

44. The Crown of Thorns
Reglerkirche, Erfurt, about 1440

45. The Trinity
Blutenburg, 1491

46. St. Lawrence. Sculpture in wood, Carlsruhe
(*photo: Karlsruhe, Badisches Landesmuseum*)

47.   Head of an Apostle by Tilman Riemenschneider.
From the Church of St. James, Rothenburg-ob-der-Tauber
(*photo: Dr. Franz Stoedtner, Düsseldorf*)

48. Madonna by Martin Schongauer. Engraving

49.   Holy Family by Dürer
Drawing.   University Library, Erlangen

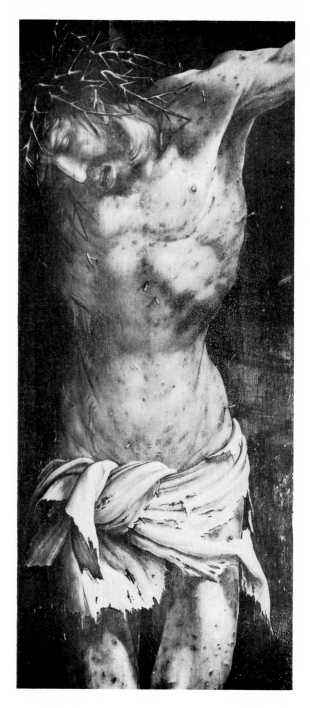

50. Matthias Grünewald. The Crucified Body
of Our Lord. From the Isenheim altar-piece
(*photo: Colmar, Musée Unterlinden*)

in the countries with a Germanic tinge and was there longest maintained, Dehio must be acknowledged to be right when he says that Gothic was not directly bound up with any national condition, but was a supernational phenomenon of the period, characteristic of the late Middle Ages, when national differences were dissolved under the glow of a consciousness of religious and ecclesiastical unity embracing the whole of European humanity.

XVIII

THE INTERIOR STRUCTURE OF
THE CATHEDRAL

" Is there not some kinship between the war waged by the Church against natural man and the way in which stone is forced by Gothic into constructions in which it is apparently oblivious of its weight, its brittleness, its natural tendency towards stratification, and in which it has apparently assumed a higher vital existence? Is there not a quite intentional contradiction to all common experience, a striving for miraculous effects, which sets as the goal to be attained by the skill of the architect the disappearance from sight of every support of the internal structure? Unquestionably, the whole of this side of Gothic, decisive as it is for the aesthetic impression, has nothing in common with the ostensible striving for constructive truth by which it seems to be controlled. Anyone incapable of discerning the considerable element of mysticism mingled with the master builders' calculations will not understand what they have to say as artists, that is to say, as true sons and legitimate spokesmen of their age."

We place these sentences of Dehio's at the head of this chapter treating of true Gothic, because they so strikingly describe the true character of all the technical advances made by Gothic, because they point out to us beforehand how the whole output of logical acumen brought to bear by the Gothic constructors in the end only serves super-logical aims.

Hardly anything new can be added to the logical and psychological interpretation of the Gothic system that has been attempted by Dehio and many others besides. So much that is intelligent and profound has already been said on the subject, that the danger of unconscious plagiarism is hardly to be avoided. Moreover, our researches are less concerned with this culmination in Gothic, than with that latent Gothic which was already expressed in the whole chain of pre-Gothic styles, the connection of which with Gothic in the narrower sense we wish in the first place to demonstrate. We may therefore be brief.

THE INTERIOR STRUCTURE OF THE CATHEDRAL

The Romanesque style was still, as we have seen, a style of masses, that is to say, the natural gravity of stone, its material entity, was still the foundation alike of the construction and of the aesthetic form. As this style had been formed under the after-suggestion of that antique feeling for architecture which had wrested from the material an organic vitality of expression, a certain process of disintegration of the material was the first necessity, in order to fit it to the Northern will to form. What remained in the Romanesque style after this disintegration was the material as such, material which had ceased to be sensuous without as yet being spiritualized. External tendencies towards the spiritualization, or rather, towards the articulation of the material, towards the liberation of the active, vital energies in it, were already present in the Romanesque style; but, as has been said, they remained merely external, they were not yet bound up with the inner construction. The first step towards this inner spiritualization is visible in the system of ribbed cross-vaulting. The first step towards actual Gothic is taken when these ribs abandon their character as a purely mimic reinforcement of expression, to assume the static control of the vaulting and to become the vehicle at one and the same time of expression and of function.

The development now beginning, however, was for the first time brought to a more pregnant and decisive issue by the introduction of the pointed arch.

It is interesting that a form which, taken purely externally, with its strong expression of activity accentuated uniformly upwards, is as it were a concise epitome in outline of the mediaeval striving for transcendentalism and consequently of the Gothic craving for expression, and which was therefore in many cases only admitted into the architectural system on purely decorative, external grounds, very soon revealed a structural applicability which at one stroke cleared the way for the structurally still restricted Gothic will to form. It is only because the decorative significance of the pointed arch coincides so completely with its structural significance, that it gained currency as the authoritative criterion of Gothic style. To be sure, the incomparably more important inner significance was thus for the most part overlooked in favour of the more obtrusive external significance. The constructive advantages of the pointed arch had naturally been known long before: the pointed arch is quite as old as the art of vaulting itself; so far, therefore, it cannot be looked upon as a Gothic discovery. But Gothic alone converted it and its constructive significance into an element of an entire system carried through with the utmost consistency.

So long as the round arch was clung to, it had been technically difficult to vault over any but square ground-plan compartments. For it was only with distances of equally wide span between the piers that equal heights could be obtained in the crowns of the vaulting. The confinement of the ground-plan to squares was therefore necessary, and this undoubtedly imparted a very grave and solemn appearance to the Romanesque building; but, on the other hand, it impeded the vertical expansion embracing both aisles and nave, which was the ambition of the Northern builder. For the only possible course was to set two small square aisle-bays alongside one square bay of the nave. A more intimate connection between the nave-vaulting and the aisle-vaulting was therefore unattainable. The rhythm of the nave and the side aisles was unequal. Where the nave took one big step, the side aisles took two small ones. Their course was therefore parallel but not concerted. Community of movement was only in a forward, not an upward direction. And as the development towards height was the peculiar aim of the Northern builder, it is clear how much it suffered from this restrictive squareness, which actually held back the uniform upward development of the building.

The focus of the early Christian basilica was the altar. With lines of compelling energy the entire attention was directed to this final goal of movement, the altar. Nor is the Gothic cathedral without its compulsion of line; but its aim is another one. Towards that imagined line, to where it vanishes into height, all its energies, all its agitation are directed. The aim of a basilica is definite, that of the Gothic cathedral indefinite. Its movement dies away into the infinite. Since in both types of building the conditions of worship in general and the practical spatial requirements remained the same, the Gothic development of height could only take effect by the side of and in spite of the lengthways development of the building demanded by the cult. The development of the building in length was therefore maintained by the oblong formation of the ground-plan of the whole. The cramped Romanesque style, with its squares rhythmically expressionless and devoid of any decided indication of direction, could not oppose to this horizontal development of the whole any equivalent, vertical development; the Gothic system, on the other hand, thanks to the pointed arch and its constructive utilization, was able to merge this great oblong of the general ground-plan, in the presence of which the Romanesque square bays were powerless in spite of all vaulting, into a system likewise made up of oblong compartments, whose longer sides did not run parallel to the longer sides of the general ground-plan, but exactly in the opposite direction. Their effect therefore was to paralyse the one-sided, longitudinal development of the building, replacing it by an equivalent development in width, which, in connection with the aims already attained in the vaulting, led to a uniform development in height. The oblong formation of the general ground-plan even proved advantageous to this vertical development. For it imparted to the whole building the character of a struggle for height, developing with redoubled energy from relatively narrow lateral limits.

This possibility of an extension in height embracing the whole of the building, including the nave and the side aisles alike—the so-called Gothic *travée* or bay—first came about, as has already been said, with the development of the pointed arch and its constructive consequences. For it was the capacity for modulation possessed by the pointed arch that first made it possible, even with unequal distances between the piers —that is, over oblong compartments of the ground-plan—to obtain vaults of equal height. The ponderous ratio, 1:2, of the arches of the nave vaulting to those of the side aisles vanishes: nave and aisles obtain the same number of vaults closely connected one with the other: they no longer run side by side towards a set goal of lengthways extension, but rise with one another upwards.

The principal accent of the whole building thus rests on the nave and its heavenward-striving movement. All else becomes subordinate to it, all else is dependent upon it. The aisles, which in the Romanesque system still acted as independent, equivalent divisions of the space, now only derive their aesthetic meaning from the movement given by the nave, to which they serve as it were only as accents. When this accentuation is still further strengthened by the introduction of two further aisles, this takes place merely in compliance with the truly Gothic need of accumulating single effects for the reinforcement of the collective impression of the whole. The nave movement, the leading theme of the whole building, is in no wise weakened by the more profuse development of the prelude; on the contrary, its great, strong lines exercise an even stronger, weightier effect by reason of the retardation, as of syncopation, set up by the side aisles.

The process of dematerializing the body of the building, which had already begun in the Romanesque style, was finally concluded by the introduction of the pointed arch into the construction of the vaulting. The Romanesque style had only attained to an external separation of the elements of static effect and those which enclosed spaces; the Gothic utterly denied those elements which were merely enclosers of space, and constructed the entire building simply and solely out of the members which were static in their effect. This movement had already manifested itself in the Romanesque period in the strengthening of the vaulting ribs, in the separation of the statically operative ribbing from the functionless inserted sectroids. The pressure of the vault was concentrated on the four corner piers supporting the vaulting, thereby removing the pressure from the walls between the piers. It was the first step on that road which ended in the complete dissolution of the wall. To a great extent it had already become a functionless filling, like the sectroids of the vault. But the strong lateral pressure exerted upon the piers by the arches which were still of semicircular span necessitated for the time being a massive construction of the piers, which did not allow the Romanesque style any final departure from the wall principle and was therefore considered by the Gothic will to form as something to be overcome. It was the introduction of the pointed arch into the vault-structure which first afforded the Gothic architect the possibility of achieving his aim of a tense and sinewy, supple, articulated building, rid of all superfluous flesh, all superfluous mass. For the much reduced lateral pressure of the pointed-arch vaulting allowed the supporting piers to be built higher and more slender, thus first making possible that thorough relaxation of the static structure, that expression of slender, supple, and burdened activity which accorded with the Gothic need for expression. It is as if, with the introduction of the pointed arch, the building were permeated by a great wave of self-awareness. The redeeming word seems to have been spoken which allowed its restrained craving for activity and its pathetic yearning for expression to find utterance. The whole building stretches itself upward in the glad consciousness of being freed from all weight of material, from all earthly confinement. The piers become high, slender, and supple: the vaulting loses itself in dizzy altitudes, and yet everything is subservient to this vaulting removed so far aloft. The entire building appears to exist only for the sake of the latter. The vaulting starts, so to speak, at the very foot of the building. All the attached shafts, great and small, rising from the ground and playing around the piers like living energies, operate both constructively and aesthetically only as a prelude to the vaulting. They hasten upwards from the ground with supple energy, to die gradually away in gentle movement. The movement of thrust from both sides is gathered into unity by a keystone at the crown of the vault, which, in spite of its actual weight conformable with its structural function as abutment, fails entirely to produce any aesthetic impression of weight, appearing rather as a natural termination light as a flower.

In this description of the Gothic interior construction, our terminology has unconsciously changed and has adopted quite a different and more sensuous tonality. We now speak of supple, vital energies, of tense sinews, of flower-like terminations—but will not the abstract, super-organic, mechanical activity of Gothic, which we have accepted as the foundation of the Northern will to art, be rendered questionable by the use of such epithets, derived from our ideas of the organic? This question must be examined, for the answer will show us that the Northern will to art aimed only at *strongly expressive* activity, and that its preference for that abstract mechanical activity was due to its vast superiority in strength of expression to organic activity, which is always connected with organic harmony, and therefore rather serves beauty than power of expression, just as a mechanically controlled marionette is more strongly expressive than a living, acting human being. On the other hand, it shows us that the Gothic will to art, when denied its abstract means of expression by external circumstances, increased the organic means of expression to the point very nearly of attaining the forcefulness of mechanical expression.

This is the position in which Gothic man finds himself in relation to the interior structure of his cathedrals.

157

Gothic man is not purely tectonic like the Greek. He is far more the fashioner of interiors, who continued and concluded the great process of the spiritualization of sensibility which had begun in Hellenistic times. Space is no longer a mere accessory in a purely tectonic process, but it is the primary, the direct starting-point of the architectural conception. For Gothic man it is now a question of wresting from this space a vitality of expression agreeing with the ideal aims of his artistic creativeness.

Now space is something in itself spiritual and incomprehensible, and so in this its essential nature it eludes every formative energy which creates expression. For no expression can be given to anything we cannot comprehend. We can only comprehend space when we take from it its abstract character, when we substitute for it our conception as of something corporeal; in short, when we turn experience of space into an experience of the senses, abstract space into real atmospheric space. Abstract space has no life, and no creative power can win from it expression; atmospheric space, on the contrary, has an inner life which acts directly upon our senses, thereby offering a foothold for our powers of formation.

Thus here in the formation of space the Gothic urge to spiritualization finds itself faced by a sphere of organic, sensuous expression. The way to its true sphere, the non-sensuous, is blocked, so the only escape is to transfer the sensuous into the super-sensuous. A super-sensuous effect had to be extracted from sensuous space experience, that is to say, the sensuous means of expression had to be increased in such a way as to result in a super-sensuous impression. Here the inner connection of Gothic with Baroque again comes to the fore. For it was this same Gothic-Mediaeval will to form which played itself out in the sensuous pathos of the Baroque, its own proper means of expression, the abstract, the super-organic, having been taken from it, in fact, by the Renaissance. Thus we find in Baroque the same sensuous-super-sensuous character as in the spatial effect of Gothic.

This specific note in Gothic space-creation and space-sensibility is made particularly clear to us, when we turn our thoughts back to the healthy, *lucid* space-sculpture in Roman architecture, as expressed, for instance, in the Pantheon. Here all pathos is lacking. The lucidity of the space-formation keeps at a distance every super-sensuous, mystic feeling. The Roman will to form, with its Classical complexion, would only allow to space a life which was organically independent, harmoniously and serenely self-contained.

To enter the Pantheon is to feel freed from individual isolation: voiceless, solemn music of space leads to a beneficent, liberating, sensuous composure: one is swayed by the unspeakably blissful rhythm of spatial life: one feels a clarification of the senses. And what more did Classical man require in all his art than this lofty bliss of ideal, sensuous clarification?

On the other hand, anyone entering a Gothic cathedral encounters something far removed from sensuous *clarification*. He encounters an *intoxication* of the senses, not that direct, gross intoxication produced by the Baroque, but a mystical intoxication of the senses which is not of this world.

Gothic space is unbridled activity. Its note is not that of solemnity or repose; it is overwhelming. It does not receive the beholder with soft gestures, but carries him violently along, acting as a mystical compulsion to which the burdened soul deems it a delight unresistingly to yield.

To be deafened in this manner by the *fortissimo* of the music of space entirely met the needs of Gothic religion and its striving for liberation. Here we are far removed from the whole classical world. To attain the mood of religion and solemnity, classical man only needed *clarity* of space. His religious and artistic bliss was closely bound up with harmony and balance. Even as a creator of space, he remained a sculptor. Gothic man, on the contrary, merely required for inducing religious feeling the pathos of space. It was only this pathos which lifted him above his earthly limitations and his inner wretchedness; it was only in that intensification of ecstasy which culminated in the annihilation of self that he could experience the awe of eternity. His inner dualism forced him as a creator of space into transcendentalism, into mysticism. Where classical man only required to be sensuously self-composed, his wish was to lose himself, to attain to the super-sensuous by self-renunciation.

Gothic man is insensible to the latent demands of atmospheric space, for beneficent, rhythmic limitation. Indeed, for the sake of his morbidly strained need for expression, he violates atmospheric life. Where classical man only listened to it and served it with understanding, he faces it aggressively. He imprisons it, places obstacle after obstacle in its path, violently wresting from it a quite definite rhythm of movement, intensified to the utmost, the aim of which is infinite height. Repelled on every side, shattered against a thousand oppositions, atmospheric life leads a tormented, agitated, restless existence within the limits of the interior, until finally, as if with an audible roar, it breaks against the vaulted roof. There a whirlwind, as it were, is formed which rises irresistibly upwards; any one at all sensitive to the impressions of space can never enter the great Gothic cathedrals without experiencing a dizziness caused by space. It is the same dizzy feeling set up by the chaotic intricacy of line in early Northern ornament. " Plus ça change, plus ça reste la même chose."

The organically rounded form of the architectural members into which the space is divided was determined by the sensuous experience of space. Everything hard or angular, which could not be reconciled with the life of atmospheric space, had to be avoided. The sensuous conception of space was transferred to the members into which it is divided. The shafts and the ribs which act as conductors to the sensuous experience are either completely round or semicircular in section; they, as well as the space they serve, possess organic expression-value. But here too the transition from the sensuous to the super-sensuous very soon occurs, that is to say, the architectural members more and more lose their bodily, material content, becoming abstract vehicles of expression. This process is completed by a conscious transformation in their profile, the first step of which is its conversion into a pear-shaped form. As the result of this conversion a more linear, more abstract expression becomes dominant within what is thoroughly corporeal in its essence. The complete elimination of corporeal analogies of expression brings the second step: the external surfaces of the profile bend inwards, leaving only a narrow fillet, flanked on both sides by a dense play of shadow, which once for all replaces the physically tangible function by a purely spiritual, intangible expressiveness. Thus here also artistic treatment ends in a non-sensuous play, which, freed from all structural aims, seems to exist merely for its own sake, a play which expresses no corporeal forces but only spiritual energies. Thus we see how even where the unavoidable sensuous conception of space on the one hand and the unavoidable static conditions on the other made inevitable an organically round and corporeally stable formation of the architectural members, the Gothic need of spiritual expression found a way for itself and spiritualized the material by a delicate process of dematerialization.

XIX

THE EXTERIOR STRUCTURE OF
THE CATHEDRAL

The Gothic cathedral is the most powerful and comprehensive presentation of mediaeval feeling. Mysticism and scholasticism, those two great forces of mediaeval life, which generally figure as incompatible opposites, are here closely united, growing directly one from the other. As the interior is all mysticism, so the exterior construction is all scholasticism. The same transcendentalism of movement unites them, merely employing different means of expression—in the one case, organically sensuous, in the other case, abstractly mechanical. The mysticism of the interior is only scholasticism intensified and guided into organic and sensuous channels.

Gottfried Semper, a slave to classical prejudices, first coined the phrase " scholasticism in stone," thinking thereby to bring Gothic into discredit. But this exactly apposite verdict on Gothic can only mean condemnation to one who, because of the narrowness of his modern, one-sided point of view, is unable to comprehend the great mediaeval phenomenon of scholasticism. We must try to break down this modern one-sidedness of judgment concerning scholasticism and endeavour to give instead of a modern relative estimation a positive interpretation. For the present, we will consider how this scholastic disposition in Northern man manifested itself architecturally.

In antique architecture, so far as it concerned itself with artistic problems of space, and in all the styles dependent upon it, more especially therefore in Romanesque, the exterior construction presented itself as the external complement of the inner limitation of space. Now we have seen that in the Gothic style the actual limits of space, that is to say, the solid walls, were dissolved and the constructive and aesthetic functions passed to the static individual forces of the structure. This fundamental alteration in the building-conception could not but exercise its natural reaction on the formation of the exterior. Here too the solid continuous walls had to be pushed aside, here too the process of emancipation of the individual forces had to be accomplished.

We saw how, in the Romanesque style, the process of dividing up the expressionless wall-surfaces began with pilaster strips and blind arcading. But the active forces, which now vitalized the walls and wrested expression from them, had only a decorative value, for as yet they had no direct visible connection with the inner construction. External forces were speaking, not the immanent forces active in the building itself. The language of construction had not yet been found, and for it alone was reserved the full power of giving form to the Gothic will for expression. The structural formation of the interior which we have seen developing as a result of the tendency to vaulting gave the signal which awakened and made independent the forces of activity latent in the outer structure of the building too. By freeing the walls from the burden of the vault and by concentrating the pressure on individual and specially accentuated points, the need for buttressing had evolved spontaneously, just as it had arisen and had been resolved in other architectures in a similar situation. The Gothic buttress system is nothing new constructively; but it was a new idea to make it visible, instead of hiding it as elsewhere in the walls enclosing the whole. In this unveiling of the buttressing lies the first aesthetic affirmation of a structural necessity, that is to say, Gothic longing for expression had simultaneously discovered in these structural necessities possibilities of aesthetic expression and found thereby the decisive principle for the exterior formation of the building.

Here too it is the introduction of the pointed arch which urges to a decision the hesitating, groping will, and as a result leads to the consistent carrying out of the system. For it was only with the introduction of the pointed arch that the vaulting of the nave reached its full height and the nave piers correspondingly their utmost slenderness, which in spite of the comparative lightness of the burden brought with it the danger of collapse. The consequent necessity of creating means of support at definite points, and that at a height at which the low side-aisles demanded by the Gothic accentuation of the nave could no longer be enlisted to receive the supporting members, led to a system of buttresses leaping freely in the air over the side aisles, that is to say, to a quite outspoken revelation of the static individual forces constituting the structure of the entire building.

With a great gesture of energy, the flying buttress carries the thrust of the nave vault on to the massive buttresses of the side aisles. To facilitate their resistance against the lateral pressure of the burden falling upon them, they are weighted down from above by pinnacles. The structural meaning of this buttress-system can therefore only be grasped when it is followed from above, downwards; but for the aesthetic impression the reverse direction is decisive, the direction from below upwards. We see how the heavenward-striving energies are released from the forces stored up in the buttresses, to attain their goal of height in a mighty, mechanical display of force. This movement from the buttresses, over the flying buttresses to the clerestory, is of compelling mimic power. All means are enlisted to force on the observer this aesthetic conception of the buttress system, which is in opposition to the structural conception. Thus the pinnacles have not the effect of a load on the buttresses but of an exuberance of energy liberated from the latter in the impulse towards height, an exuberance which shoots impatiently upwards even before the true aim of the upward development has been attained. Owing to this, so to speak, useless upward soaring of energy in the pinnacles, the movement of the flying buttress, after this delay, unswerving in its certainty and fully conscious of its aim, acquires a still more intense and convincing power of expression.

From the purely structural point of view, the position is that the secrets of the free, elastic, structurally incomprehensible formation of the Gothic interior betray themselves to anyone stepping outside the building by a laboured medley of struts and props, upon which the building must lean in order to achieve its spatial effects; structurally, therefore, the exterior has the effect of a sobering disclosure of the bewildering formation of the interior. Nevertheless the aesthetic impression suggested to the observer by every possible means is that the upward movement of the interior is merely repeated by these architectural members of the exterior. The incomprehensible rhythmic movement of space seems to have been petrified from within on the outer surface. The upward striving energies, which in the interior have not yet come to rest, seem to press outwards, in order to lose themselves, freed from all limitation and confinement, in the infinite. In ceaselessly renewed onsets they swarm around the core of the interior, striving then to soar to the infinite beyond it.

A kind of exterior bay is attained. A united extension of the building, both aisles and nave included, towards an ideal height now becomes visible in the exterior of the structure also. The same transcendental movement of expression, which, in the interior, expresses itself in soft, supple lines, here reveals itself in a harsh activity of tremendous mechanical expressiveness, directing a thousand energies towards the same object.

We have seen how, in the formation of the interior, the development in height was still restricted by adherence to the old basilica scheme, dictated by requirements of cult, the significance of which lay in the altar space. For the urge to ideal movement of Gothic man, this precisely accentuated movement in the direction of the altar was too confined. He sought to counteract this horizontal movement by a vertical development which would open for him the way to the infinite. The bays are applied like brakes to the horizontal movement to divert its energies upwards. But all this vertical development in the interior still lacked its final consummation. It was only counter-movement, not conquest. It could not undisputedly give to itself the decisive accent, for this accent was prescribed to it by the cult. The interior was not able, was not allowed, to detach itself from the altar.

For this limitation in the interior, the Gothic architect derived compensation in the construction of the exterior. Here Gothic will to form, freed from all considerations of cult, could be allowed to speak, and the result was the formation of the towers as the principal accent of the entire exterior. The emancipation from the old basilica scheme, with its movement towards the altar, is here entirely carried through in favour of an ideal vertical development. A movement in a directly contrary sense is here expressed. For the external effect of the horizontal body of the building is merely that of a preparation, merely an upbeat towards the great triumphant movement of the towers. It is from all the strainings of energy expressed in the flying-buttress system of the body of the building that the easy, natural upward development of the tower system first receives its ultimate dynamic. All the individual energies that play and wear themselves out on the exterior are as it were gathered together and united, in order to find their liberating utterance in the ideal architectural structure of the towers which is untrammelled by any purpose. Like a transfigured apotheosis of Gothic transcendentalism, the towers put the final touch to the whole building, and there is no one stone in it which does not serve the purpose of the whole. Nowhere is the Gothic " self-intoxication by logical formalism " more purely expressed than here, but nowhere is the super-logical, transcendental effect of this logical work of multiplication stamped with such a monumental and convincing character. A critic who is prejudiced in favour of the classical may have no feeling for this super-logical effect: he sees the means only and misses the aim. He merely perceives the expenditure in logical sagacity without understanding the super-logical wherefore of this expenditure; in short, this petrified scholasticism can only appear to him a methodical madness. But anyone who has learned to know the Gothic will to form, and has followed its evolution from the chaotic intricacy of early ornament to this deliberate chaos of energy developed in stone, sees his Classical standards destroyed by the grandeur of this expression: and, filled with forebodings, he realizes the mighty world of mediaeval sensibility, torn as it was by extremes and therefore capable of supernatural exertions of energy; and so long as he is influenced by the overwhelming impression of this exalted Gothic hysteria, he is almost inclined to be unjust towards the healing process of the Renaissance, which brought the feverish Gothic sensibility back to a normal—one might almost say *bourgeois*—temperature, replacing the grandeur of pathos with the ideal of beauty and serene repose.

We spoke of the architectural multiplication revealed in the construction of the tower system. It is the same character of multiplication already observed in early ornament. There too we saw that the individual motive is multiplied by itself, in contrast with the character of addition shown in Classical ornament. And here too in architecture the denominator of this process of multiplication is the denominator of infinity, causing as the final result of the logical process a chaotic confusion.

But Gothic man seeks to lose himself not only in the infinity of the great, but also in the infinity of the small. The infinity of movement which is macrocosmically expressed in the architectural structure as a whole expresses itself microcosmically in every smallest detail of the building. Every individual detail is, in itself, a world of bewildering activity and infinity, a world which repeats in miniature, but with the same means, the expression of the whole, compelling the same unresisting surrender and inducing the same effect of stupefaction. The crown of a pinnacle is a cathedral in miniature, and anyone who has sunk himself in the ingenious chaos of a tracery can here experience on a small scale the same thrill in logical formalism as he experiences in the building system as a whole. The unity of the will to form, with its unfailing accomplishment, is astounding.

We are unwilling to conclude these by no means exhaustive investigations of Gothic architecture without making one fact clear. We have purposely avoided adducing any particular building of the Gothic epoch as an example and document; neither have we gone into details of the various periods of Gothic in the narrower sense. A purely psychological investigation of style must rather keep in view the ideal type only, an ideal which may perhaps never have been realized, but which has loomed ahead as the immanent goal of all real endeavours. Here, therefore, it is not a question of this or that monument of Gothic architecture, but of the idea of Gothic which, by the recognition of the characteristic Gothic will to form, we have sought to distil out of the fullness of its realizations in all their wealth of variations and shades.

XX

THE PSYCHOLOGY OF SCHOLASTICISM

Scholasticism is in the sphere of religion what Gothic architecture is in the sphere of art. It is an equally eloquent proof of the exalted hysteria of the Middle Ages, and has in the same way been misconstrued, owing to the fact that a false standard was applied to it. The misunderstandings concerning scholasticism are identical with those concerning Gothic architecture.

In it a display of logical sagacity was also supposed to exist, the inner super-logical aim of which was not comprehended. The external aim of scholastic speculation was the only point considered, that is to say, the intention to provide reason with a justification of the system of ecclesiastical dogma. It has been observed in tones of reproach that scholasticism did not set out to discover any truth as yet unknown, but contented itself with supporting on grounds of reason, and proving to be rational, the truth already comprised in the theological-philosophical system of the church—which, inwardly, rests on divine revelation, outwardly on the authority of Aristotle. Scholasticism was supposed to be merely a handmaiden of theology. The entire display of logical sagacity therefore was only the result of the complicated nature of the task, which consisted in bringing within the range of the understanding facts of revelation and faith which evaded the direct explanation and justification demanded by the understanding. This led to logical subtlety, to the involved sophistical dialectics of scholasticism. Nothing was seen in scholastic speculation but the hair-splitting arguments and logical quibbles of a lawyer, desirous of winning a lost cause by all the arts of sham logic.

On the other hand, anyone who has recognized that latent scholasticism which betrays itself long before the actual historical scholasticism, and without any connection with the Christian doctrine of salvation, in the peculiarly involved, restless, and complicated course of Northern thought

169

in general: he who has recognized, for instance, the connection between riddles, " that favourite form of Germanic dialogue " (Lamprecht), with their involved agility, evading any clearness, any direct road, and the involved dialectic of scholasticism, finds himself forced to a conception of scholasticism which entirely ignores its external theological aims and keeps its eyes upon the character of the thought alone. As in these riddles and the answering of them, the display of logic and sagacity has no sort of relationship to the occasion and the result, so in scholasticism proper, the direct theological aim need hardly be taken into consideration in comparison with the joy of a certain involved, contorted movement of thought as such. On the analogy of artistic will to form, one might therefore speak of an intellectual will to form, that is to say, of the will to a definite form of thought which exists quite independently of the special problem. The object of thought would thus hardly come into consideration as against the definite impulse to intellectual activity. Just as Northern man was seized by a mania for artistic construction and building, going far beyond all practical requirements, so he was seized also by a mania for intellectual construction which betrays the same need of becoming engrossed in a self-created activity of an abstract kind, whether logical or mechanical. The primary impulse in Northern intellect was not for knowledge but for movement. This impulse for movement was utilized at first without any direct object: it is, so to speak, the ornamental stage of thought as expressed in the asking of riddles referred to above, and in a thousand other forms. Now as in art the Northern impulse for purely ornamental form was required, owing to the development of architecture, to undertake a direct task, a task which did not grow out of itself, but was imposed upon it from without, namely, the remodelling of the antique basilica scheme, so on the intellectual side also, thought indulged in merely for its own sake was set a task, imposed upon it from without by the acceptance of Christianity and its consequences, in the accomplishment of which it revealed its highest capabilities. And, just as the Gothic cathedral goes far beyond its direct aim, the creation of space, creating, by the addition of the tower to the exterior, a monument which almost approaches the same degree of ideal aimlessness manifested in the ornament, so scholastic thought also outruns the direct occasion of its activity, developing into an autonomous revelation of an abstract movement of thought, free from any purpose.

It cannot therefore be said that scholasticism wished to approach the Divine by means of intellectual knowledge. It desired far more to participate in the Divine by means of its manner of thinking, this intricate movement of thought so chaotic yet in its logic so deliberate. It was not the result of thought, but the abstract process of the movement of thought, which bred in the scholastic that intellectual ecstasy which stupefied and liberated him,—in the same way as the abstract process of movement in the line, which he made visible in ornament, or in the same way as the abstract process of movement in the energies of stone, which he made visible in architecture. It is *one* definite will to form, which governs all these manifestations, causing them to produce identical resultant phenomena in spite of their material differences. It is the same self-intoxication by logical formalism, the same expenditure of rational means for a super-rational purpose, the same methodical madness, the same deliberate chaos. And this similarity of results must argue a community of principle. This common principle is no other than Gothic transcendentalism, which, born of a vague, confused dualism, can only find appeasement and liberation in states of hysteria, in convulsive excitement, in overstrained pathos.

We have seen then that in mediaeval philosophy everything is bound up with the abstract process of the act of thinking, in the same manner as in mediaeval painting everything is bound up with the abstract line and its specific expression. Just as in mediaeval painting everything represented is merged into the higher life of the means of representation, so also in scholastic philosophy every direct purpose of knowledge merges into the higher life of the means of knowledge, and its autonomous activity. It was a catastrophe which gave a wrong direction to all mediaeval thought and threw it out of its course when, owing to the Renaissance, thought, which till then had been an end in itself, was degraded to a mere means to an end, namely, the knowledge of external scientific truth, when the *purpose* of knowledge became everything and the *process* of knowledge nothing. Thought then lost its abstract autonomy and became a servant; it became the slave of truth. Formerly, it had occupied itself as it were without an object, finding its delight only in its own activity, for, by belief in the revealed divine truth, it had been spared every actual impulse directed towards knowledge of the unknown; but now an actual object, the truth, was set before it; now it was required to renounce its own autonomy and to receive all its laws simply and solely from that object. In short, it was condemned to be a mere intellectual copy of the true, that is to say, of objective facts—like the line in painting, which also had once lived by its own particular expression alone, and now, in the same circumstances, also lost its autonomous, arabesque existence to become a limiting outline, a reproduction of the world of natural forms, a mere handmaid of the objective. As the new Renaissance conception of scientific truth was bound up with experiment, so the new Renaissance conception of artistic truth was bound up with anatomical study. In both cases, objective truth became an ideal, which means that a firm foothold had been found in this world: and thus transcendentalism in artistic and intellectual creation was at an end. The Renaissance brought about the great healing process, the great process of the vulgarization of sensibility, which swept away all mediaeval abnormalities and for the power of the supernatural substituted the beauty of the natural.

XXI

THE PSYCHOLOGY OF MYSTICISM

Just as in the Gothic cathedral mysticism and scholasticism are indissolubly united, and directly evolved the one from the other, so they are quite closely united and intertwined in the actual facts of history. Their bond of union, that which makes them phenomena of similar quality, is their transcendental character. The line of demarcation is found in their differing means of expression, which naturally are not arbitrary, but rest on inner foundations determined by important changes in the sensibility of Northern man, with which therefore in this connection we must now concern ourselves.

Just as we are conscious of the interior of a Gothic cathedral as a super-sensuous experience arising out of the sensuous, which by its whole nature is in direct contrast with the abstract world of expression of Gothic exterior architecture and the means by which it affects us, so we feel the difference between mysticism and scholasticism as being determined by the more sensuous tinge of mysticism, as contrasted with the abstract, non-sensuous nature of scholasticism. Instead of the intellectual exaltation in which the religious feeling of scholasticism sought its certainty of salvation, we see, in mysticism, emotional rapture becoming the measure of religious experience. Mental rapture is converted into a spiritual rapture. But spiritual experience, like spatial experience, is something apart from everything intellectual and abstract, something that is directly fed by our senses. For what we call spiritual is only the intensification and refinement of sensuous feeling until it has reached the sphere of the super-sensuous. And so, when it is no longer the mind which soars up to God, as in scholasticism, but the soul, it indicates that in religious life a growth in sensuousness has come about. And this growth in the sensuousness of feeling, in view of the whole trend of the inquiry dominating our investigations, is an extraordinarily important phenomenon from which we can draw decisive conclusions.

For wherever in the inner process of man's development we detect an increase in the sensuousness of feeling, we know that an alleviation of the relation, at first strongly dualistic, between man and the outer world, has so far set in that the individual man dares to separate himself from the crowd, and to face the outer world alone. For abstractness of feeling is nothing but the result of subjection to the crowd. The feeling of the coherent crowd, still undifferentiated as individuals, is of necessity abstract, for its coherence, its fear of a relaxation of that cohesion, betokens that it is still far too much oppressed by a dualistic anxiety and consequently oppressed also by an urge towards liberation; that abstract values with their superhuman, fatalistic character of necessity can alone give it rest and appeasement. Crowd sensibility and abstract sensibility are indeed two words for the same thing. And it is equally tautological to say that, with the awakening of the individual consciousness, the abstractness of sensibility was relaxed and transformed into sensuousness. For the abstract is precisely the impersonal, the super-personal, and, as such, an expression of the undifferentiated crowd, while sensuous feeling is inseparably bound up with the process of the individualization of humanity, and can only be experienced by individual personalities. The man who has been set free from the crowd feels of necessity sensuously and naturally, because his detachment from the crowd proves precisely that dualism has to a certain extent vanished, and a certain feeling of unity between man and the outer world has set in. It is true that the crowd can feel sensuously, but only the crowd composed of individual personalities; not the crowd still individually undifferentiated which was the vehicle of feeling in the Middle Ages.

The dualistic relationship of fear between man and the outer world had therefore first to be relaxed, the instinctive consciousness of the unfathomableness of existence had to ebb away before man could dare to face alone this existence, that is to say, the infinite world of phenomena. The growing feeling for personality means the decay of the feeling for the great world. Thus we see that Oriental man never took part in the European process of individualization. His feeling for the world, that is to say, his knowledge of the deceptiveness of the world of appearances and of the unfathomableness of existence, is too firmly rooted in his instinct. His feeling and his art therefore remained abstract. But in the development of Northern humanity, which was in bondage to dualism, but not chastened by it, a marked decrease of dualism resulted from the growing certainty of external knowledge; consequently a certain process of individualization followed, the vague, inadequate character of which we must by no means ignore, for it was at any rate decisive for the increase in sensuous feeling, observable in mysticism. We see that in mysticism personal spiritual experience becomes the vehicle of divine knowledge, and this shows us that, in the relationship of Northern man to the world, a change of temperature has taken place; there has been a gain in warmth and confidence. There is something quite new and extraordinary in the mediaeval conception that the Divine should no longer be sought in non-sensuous abstractions, beyond all things earthly and human, in a realm of supernatural inevitability, but in the focus of one's own ego, in the mirror of inward contemplation, in the ecstasy of spiritual rapture. It is with a quite new human self-consciousness, with a quite new human pride, that the poor human ego deems itself worthy to become a vessel of God. Thus mysticism is nothing else than the belief in the divinity of the human soul, for it is only because the soul itself is divine that it can see God. " The soul as Microtheos, God in miniature, is the solution of all the riddles of mysticism " (Windelband). How far removed such an arrogant point of view is from all Oriental transcendentalism! How far the latter is removed from the faith that what is human, limited, accidental, could so expand as to participate in the Divine, the unlimited, the absolute! The Oriental knows that in his finiteness, he can never see God. His God lives only beyond the confines of humanity. But the mystic—and no self-renunciation on his part can deceive us as to this—believes that he can already in this world have a share in the Beyond. While he reduces that great Beyond—that Beyond which lies behind all that is human and living—to a personal Beyond, that is to say, to a Beyond only to be attained by mere self-denial; whilst therefore he descends from denial of the world to denial of self, he unconsciously draws nearer to the actual world and its sensuous sphere. A relaxation of transcendental feeling has begun, which manifests itself on every side in the very nature of mysticism. The principle of divine transcendence gradually sinks into the conception of divine immanence. Mysticism has become so near to earth, that it believes the Divine to be no longer outside the world, but contained in the world, that is to say, in the

human soul and all that is accessible to it. It believes that it can participate in it by the way of inward rapture and self-absorption.

With this conception of the Divinity of the human soul, a warm wave
of tender sensuousness flooded the stern Northern world. For into the
circle of experience of spiritual sensibility was drawn, not only the Divine,
but also the natural. While mysticism converts man into a vessel of the
Divine, while it suffers both God and the world to be reflected in the
same mirror of the human soul, it initiates a process of beatification, a
process of divinization, or, to give it its correct name, a process of human-
izing the things belonging to the external world and to nature, a process
which consistently develops into that idealistic Pantheism which claims
as its brothers trees and animals, in short, every created thing.

The certainty of being able to see God in oneself leads to a springtime
of the soul, and this springtime reacts on the whole world of existence,
which is reflected in the soul. It is a refined, subtle anthropomorphism,
an anthropomorphism become spiritual, which here expresses itself.
As in this case it is not the clear senses in which the world of existence is
mirrored but the soul, that super-sensuous element, this process of
sensualization of the world of existence initiated by mysticism is not of
such a clear, sensuous nature as that of Antiquity and of the Renaissance:
it would in this case be more accurate to speak of a process of spiritualization than of a process of sensualization. But in the close connexion
between sensuous and spiritual feeling, it is clear that none the less this
new, mystical feeling formed a connecting link with that refined, sensuous
feeling which was established by the Renaissance as the European ideal.

With mysticism, therefore, the sensuous element makes its appearance
in Gothic, although at first it was so slight and subtle that it manifests
itself merely as super-sensuousness. This sensuous-super-sensuousness
of advanced Gothic is best described as the lyrical element of Gothic.
The springtime of the soul becomes the springtime of the senses, the
delight in the ego, a delight in nature, and a world of lyric exuberance
is awakened. It is the most intimate, most delicate drama which the
evolution of Gothic offers to our observation, to watch how this new
lyric element in Gothic makes a compromise with the old, rigid, non-
naturalistic will to form proper to its constitution, gradually clothing with
bud and blossom the rigid world of abstract forms. At first, there is a

shy play round the old rigid forms, then a more intimate cajolery, until finally they are completely merged in a charming, lyrically tinged naturalism. The capitals become flowery wonders, there is no end to the luxuriance of creeping tendrils, and the tracery, once so formally and geometrically planned, develops into a marvellous world of bud and blossom. Within the chaos of stiff lines there now develops a chaos of bloom. Thus ornament also travels the road from the abstract scholasticism of its early period to the sensuous-super-sensuous mysticism of the late Gothic period.

The plastic arts also, in the narrower sense of the term, shared in this lyrical delight in nature, in the flooding of the world of existence with the warm waves of spiritual sympathy. It is not to the coarse world of facts that the mystic in his loving fervour abandons himself, but to a spiritually transfigured world, a world entirely immersed in tender, lyrical sensibility. All rigidity melts, all that is hard becomes soft, every line is saturated with spiritual feeling. A smile dawns on the stern features of the statues, a smile which is born from within and seems the reflection of an inward blessedness. Everything is transformed into lyricism, inwardness, and spirituality. Nature, known to scholasticism only as a hard actuality and therefore denied by it, now becomes the garden of God; it breaks into blossom and turns from hard actuality to tender idyll. The hard, rigid outlines of the characteristic drawing grow soft. Rhythmically smooth calligraphy is substituted for crinkly angularity. The intellectually expressive lines become spiritually expressive lines, the intellectual energy of the linear expression ebbs away into calligraphic intricacy. What is lost in greatness is gained in beauty.

XXII

INDIVIDUALITY AND PERSONALITY

It would need a special account, going into every intimate detail, to demonstrate this delightful and varied counterplay and interplay of scholasticism and mysticism, of super-personally abstract and personally natural feeling in Gothic art. For the present, as we are only considering the main lines of development, the hints given in the preceding chapter must suffice. In this chapter, however, we have yet to examine the relation of mysticism to the Renaissance.

We have seen that the increase of sensuousness in feeling, which coincides with the appearance of mysticism, is connected with the process of individualization in Northern man. In religion, as well as in art, we have seen how the individual ego became the vehicle of feeling in place of the crowd. Mediaeval feeling was identical with abstract feeling, that is to say, the feeling of the crowd, and therefore it would appear that with mysticism the way was prepared for modern developments. Indeed, there can be no doubt on this point: it is the history of modern sensibility, the history of modern art, which begins with mysticism.

He who detects the presence of the Renaissance in mysticism is therefore not deceived, only he must never forget that mysticism is a Northern product and that the Renaissance came from the South. Neither must he overlook the differences lying behind what is common to both. Mysticism leads to Protestantism, the Southern Renaissance to European classicism.

It is just the elementary difference between Northern and Southern humanity which leads to quite different goals two movements identical in their starting-point. The common starting-point of both movements is the transference of feeling and knowledge from the crowd to the individual ego: and with this we are up against Burckhardt's clear-cut dictum as to the discovery of the individual by the Renaissance. A certain rectification of this dictum will show us the right way and make intelligible to us the distinction between the Northern and the Southern development.

The rectification demanded in Burckhardt's saying is the substitution of " personality " for the word " individual." For it was personality that was revealed in the Southern Renaissance, which Burckhardt had in mind, whilst the conception of the individual belongs to the Northern world; it corresponds exactly to the inmost essence of Northern mysticism.

For the word " individual " has a negative complexion which makes it totally unsuited to describe the Southern phenomenon. Owing to its etymological genesis, it of necessity calls forth the idea of a mechanical parcelling out of a crowd into its very smallest indivisible component parts. This mechanical process of subdivision which delivers over to incoherence the individual separate parts, gives no picture of the process of development enacted in the Southern Renaissance. For here there was no crowd mechanically divided up into innumerable, incoherent, individual parts, but a vast social organism, gradually becoming conscious of its individual parts and developing its compact mass into a thousand delicate, individual organs, each one of which lived in a smaller, more subtle way the life which held the whole organism together. It was therefore no mechanical process of division, but an organic process of differentiation which guaranteed organic coherence in spite of all differentiation. For this, quite positive, process of development, the negative complexion of the word " individual " is totally unsuited; the word " personality " as commonly used is the right one.

To the Northern process of individualization which came about with mysticism, the negative complexion of the word is all the more appropriate. In reality this was rather a process of disintegration, a crumbling away of a compact mass into innumerable self-willed individual parts, withdrawing from one another and abandoning all concentric organic coherence. Northern man feels also the negative character of this process of individualization, that is to say, he immediately becomes conscious of his individual isolation: for by the renunciation of that ego to which he has attained, he seeks to free himself from individual isolation. The Southern Renaissance movement with its awakening consciousness of personality leads to self-assertion, self-affirmation, self-control. The Northern process of individualization led, on the contrary, to self-denial, to self-contempt. In the latter case the individual being is considered as something negative, even actually sinful. The individualism of mysticism preaches: Annihilate your individuality. Or, as mystical language expresses it: " Trample self under foot. He who persists in himself cannot know God." That is the peculiar state of discord in mysticism: born of individualism, it immediately preaches against its own origin. Whilst the man of the Renaissance becomes aware of his ego and conscious of his personality, to become inwardly quite free and independent and to receive the world as his own with undismayed self-assertion, Northern man only becomes aware of his ego immediately to abandon it again in fervent seeking after God. He has, in fact, become only an individual, not a personality. Thus mysticism, like scholasticism, remains transcendental, and in both the ecstatic element and the need for liberation play the same part. The process of individualization does not allow the dualistic disunion to disappear: it merely permits it to assume different forms.

If, therefore, we recognize mysticism as a movement in a certain sense parallel to the Southern Renaissance, we must not of course misunderstand this transcendental character which separates it from all classical healthiness and worldliness of feeling, and makes of it a purely Gothic product. For Gothic was the name we gave to that great phenomenon irreconcilably opposed to the classical, a phenomenon not bound to any single period of style, but revealing itself continuously through all the centuries in ever new disguises: a phenomenon not belonging to any age but rather in its deepest foundations an ageless racial phenomenon, deeply rooted in the innermost constitution of Northern man, and, for this reason, not to be uprooted by the levelling action of the European Renaissance.

In any case we must not understand race in the narrow sense of racial purity: here the word race must include all the peoples, in the composition of which the Germans have played a decisive part. And that applies to the greater part of Europe. Wherever Germanic elements are strongly present, a racial connection in the widest sense is observable, which, *in spite of* racial differences in the ordinary sense, is unmistakably operative, and which is as it were established and recorded for all time in historical phenomena like Gothic. For the Germans, as we have seen, are the *conditio sine qua non* of Gothic. They introduce among self-confident peoples that germ of sensuous uncertainty and spiritual distractedness from which the transcendental pathos of Gothic then surges so irrepressibly upwards.

To disclose the latent Gothic existing before true Gothic, this was the real purpose of this sketch. To establish the existence of this latent Gothic after true Gothic down to our own times another book would be needed. In spite of non-Gothic means of expression, the Gothic character is still quite plainly visible in Baroque. To reveal the manner in which the latent Gothic made its appearance later, much finer and more delicate tools would be required than those we have found adequate for the present enquiry. For the processes of disguise undergone by this latent Gothic naturally become ever more differentiated and more subtle; and who knows whether, in some such new investigation, penetrating to the inmost secret cells of the phenomena of style, much Northern classicism of recent times may not after all reveal itself as merely Gothic in disguise?